FABRICS AND THREADS FOR SCHOOLS

About the book

There is such a wide variety of fabrics and threads available today that there is no excuse for any child, girl or boy, of any age, to be bored during periods devoted to needlecraft. However, it is important that children should be given careful guidance as to the use of these materials and much of the success depends on the ability of the teacher to convey his or her knowledge and enthusiasm to the class.

With the right approach even the most stubborn child can be coaxed into producing an interesting and creative piece of work of which he is justly proud.

In order to help the busy teacher to prepare an interesting and worthwhile programme which is also of real educational value to the class, Anne Coleman has been persuaded to write this book so that the ideas which she herself has proved to be so valuable may be shared by others.

She has used a simple yet effective formula, ideal for the primary and middle schools, although nonetheless effective in the upper school, which can be adapted to the needs of the individual teacher and class. The material is clearly arranged for easy reference. On each page there is a wealth of ideas in the form of brief notes, clear diagrams and photographs.

Children themselves find great pleasure in collecting remnants of fabrics and threads so even when the school budget is low this is one time when stocks of suitable materials can be high.

FABRICS AND THREADS FOR SCHOOLS

Anne Coleman

Photographs by Alan J Oates

B T BATSFORD LIMITED   LONDON

First published 1977
ISBN 0 7134 0187 7

Filmset by
Servis Filmsetting Ltd
Manchester
Printed in Great Britain by
The Anchor Press Ltd, Tiptree, Essex
for the publishers
B T Batsford Ltd
4 Fitzhardinge Street
London W1H 0AH

CONTENTS

ACKNOWLEDGMENT

I would like to thank Mrs M Dalloway, senior adviser in design and social education to Avon County Council, for all her help and advice and also other members of the department, particularly Graeme Alexander, schools art adviser; the heads, staffs and children of Crossways Junior School, Thornbury – Stoke Lodge Junior School, Patchway – Deerswood Infant and Junior School, Kingswood – Whitehall Junior School, Bristol – Backwell Comprehensive School, who tried out the ideas, often with no previous experience of embroidery, collage or weaving; Mrs Pat White for help with some technical details; my daughters Philippa and Caroline and some of their friends and neighbours, Caroline, Alison, Jane, Sarah, Fiona and Cecile; and Peter Coleman for advice and much encouragement.

A C Bristol 1977

INTRODUCTION

Since the war, a revolution has occurred in embroidery which has changed it almost beyond recognition. The edges between embroidery and weaving have blurred and, in some cases, disappeared. Fabric collage has grown and flourished with the advent of good adhesives and the tremendous variety of new fabrics. Knitting, crochet, lace and macramé are incorporated with stitches. Embroidery can mean anything which is constructed of fabric and thread and might also include other substances such as wood and metal, papier mâché and perspex.

There are many reasons for this change, which has also occurred in other crafts, as artists and craftsmen borrow ideas and techniques from one another. The shortages of war first forced craftsmen to experiment with alternative materials. The war itself broke down many conventions in all fields. Immigration, foreign travel and the influence of other cultures, particularly through television, widened the horizons of the craftsman. A more liberal and free education system, more leisure and more money have made young people eager and confident to try out new ideas.

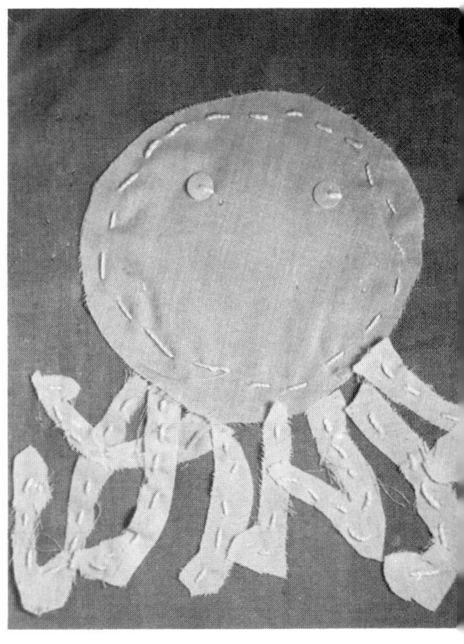

1 Appliqué. Granville (10)

One result of this upheaval is modern embroidery. It is based on the same stitches and even the same techniques as before, but used in a different way. It is as if a kaleidoscope has been shaken. The bits are the same but the pattern has changed.

In school, whatever the age of the child, one of the most important things is to experiment with fabric and thread to see what effects can be achieved. Fabric is a flexible medium. It can be twisted, plaited, pleated, gathered and rolled. Stitches can be used to make lines and also to cover whole areas. Different threads can be used on a variety of backgrounds to give exciting textures. Embroidery gives experience of a tremendous variety of surfaces and as much guided experiment as possible should be offered to a child.

It is not necessary to learn a large number of different or complicated stitches. It is much more important to find out what one stitch will do when used with varied threads on different fabrics.

IDEAS FOR DESIGN

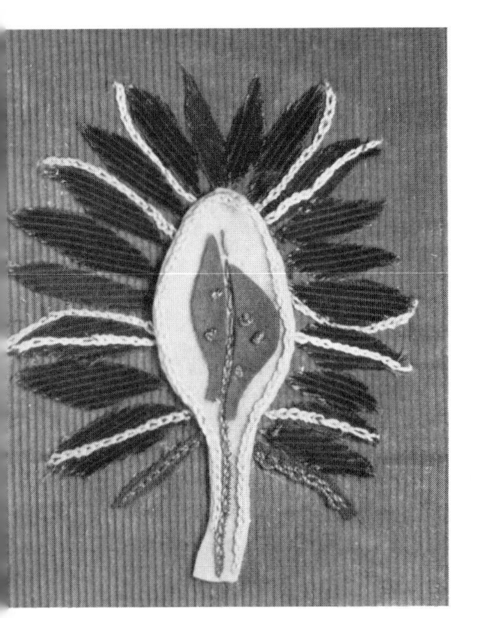

2 *Appliqué. Sally (11)*

The ideas given in this book are intended to enrich the things which children make in fabric and thread. They can be tried out by themselves, or in a larger individual or class project. It is very important to have careful preliminary discussions with the child, the group or the class about the project in hand. This prompts the imagination and brings to mind forgotten detail. The fabric and thread will make the design, so these must be chosen with great thought and care. Time must also be given to talking about suitable colours and textures. The feel or texture of a piece of embroidery is just as important as the colour. These ideas for designs to use in embroidery are not just for hangings and pictures, but for puppets and toys, tote bags and cushions, headbands, boxes, screens, jeans, other items of clothing and jewellery.

Design based on geometric form

One can begin with a dot. An extended dot makes a line. A curved line makes a spiral or a circle. Several circles can be arranged in rows, clusters, overlapping and scattered to make patterns. Some circles can be large, some can be small. A dot is a small circle. Big circles can enclose smaller circles. Circles and dots can be made with stitches, or fabric or both. A circle can be cut up in a variety of ways. The pieces can be arranged and rearranged, then rearranged again.

Similar experiments can be done with straight lines, which make rectangles, triangles, diamonds and stars. It is interesting to note the different effect of the straight line patterns and the curved line patterns.

Design based on people

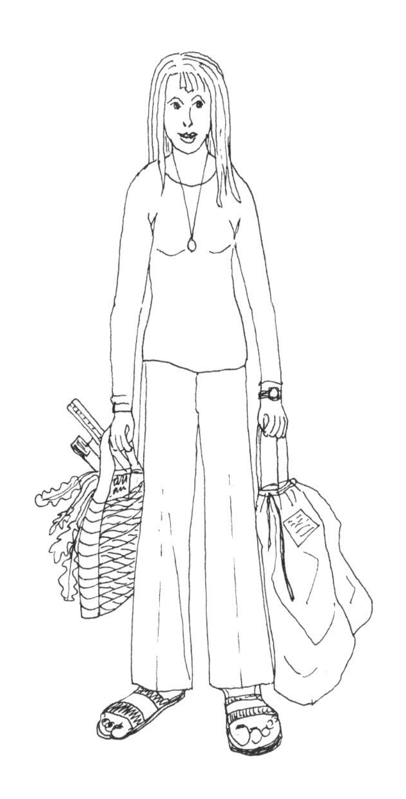

Children enjoy making self portraits. They should be given the opportunity of looking in a handmirror to see themselves. They are then reminded of the colour of their hair, skin, eyes; the texture of the eyelashes, eyebrows and hair; the shape of teeth, lips, ears and chin. They should compare similarities and differences. From the self portrait the child can progress to other known people such as parents and relations, teachers, friends, policemen, dustmen, milkmen, etc.

A picture can be based on the sort of activity one person can do when alone, for example riding a bike, reading a book, driving a car, playing the piano or violin, taking the dog for a walk.

Children might go on to discuss what two people might do together; riding a tandem, playing a duet, playing tennis, giving someone a pick-a-back, combing someone's hair.

From two people, progress to a few people or a crowd and what they might do, for example at a football match, in a traffic jam, at a strike meeting, waiting in a queue, at a picnic, at a riot, or in an orchestra.

This division of people into one or two, a few or a crowd gives a wide variety of activity which might be used in finding ideas for designs in embroidery.

3 Quilting. Jayne (10)

Design based on places and happenings

Places where children and young people go can give great scope for lively pictures; this includes festivities such as Christmas, bonfire night, rolling Easter eggs, rag day processions and the fair. Apart from school itself, children go to shops, bus stations, railway stations, boating on the river, in a car on the motorway, visiting factories, concerts, etc. It is important to remember that these places include people, and that a picture can look very empty without them.

Design based on animals, birds, fish, reptiles

Many children keep a pet or help to look after creatures at school. They are able to see how the animals live and feed, how they move, and observe their pattern and texture. Perhaps it is possible to arrange a visit to a zoo or aquarium or a farm, to see more exotic animals and birds, and also to see animals with their young.

Children are interested in animals, and like to take note of shape and dimensions. Is the animal hairy, or furry, or woolly, smooth or leathery? Has it whiskers, a tail, ears, claws, a pattern, many teeth? Insects, butterflies, spiders, moths and beetles all make excellent designs. Collections of insects can still be found in some museums as well as those seen in the environment.

Design based on natural form

In the countryside it is easy to find flowers, leaves and stones on which to base designs, but even in an urban setting, dandelions grow in the most unlikely places, moss and lichens grow on stones and tree barks, even if they have taken on the black colour of the surrounding soot. Beautiful and unusual patterns can be found in autumn leaves, snowflakes seen through a microscope and puddles of rainwater in the kerbside. The wind blows the trees and the clouds, and water makes patterns on the sand. Oil dripping in a puddle gives a rainbow effect.

4 Appliqué. Dean (9)

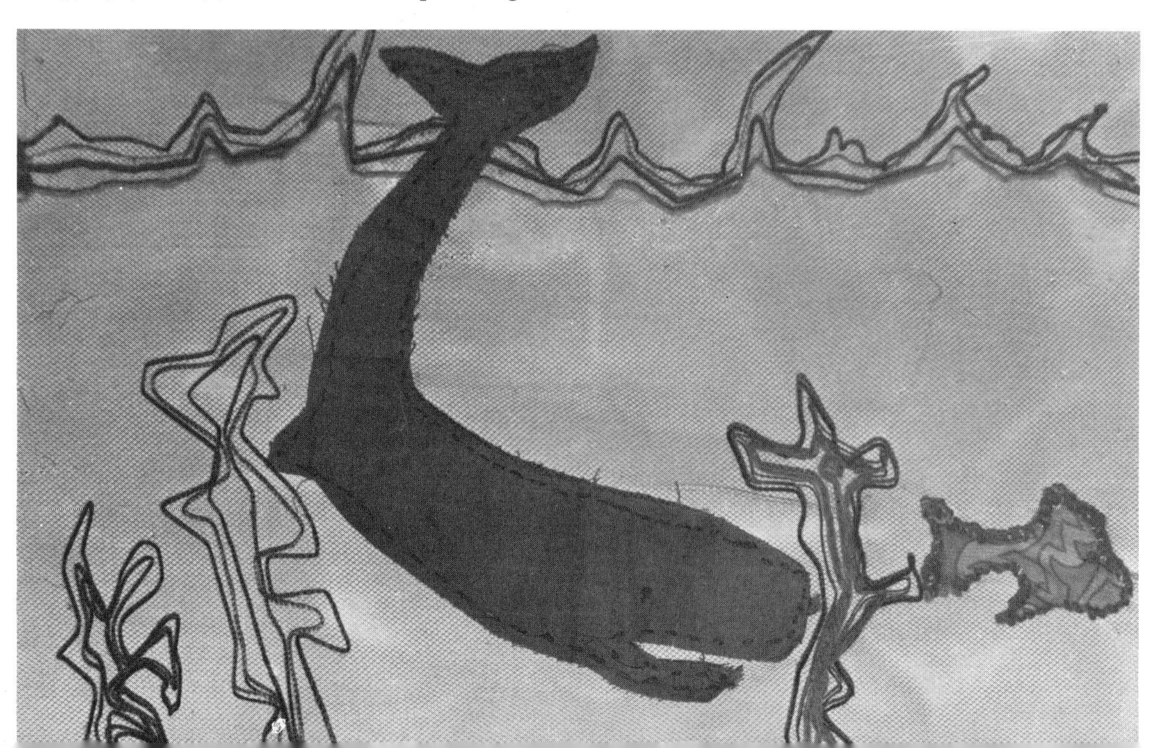

Design based on man-made patterns

Our environment is overflowing with man-made patterns which can be incorporated into embroidery. Those made by bricks, paving stones and cobbles; by fences, railings and walls. There are rows of windows, groups of chimneys, shapes of roofs, silhouettes of churches, bridges, cranes and towers. Rows of cars stand by the kerbside, rows of cups hang in a cupboard, tins are piled in pyramids in shops, sweets and chocolates are arranged in ranks on counters. Washing on a line, machinery glimpsed through a workshop door, scaffolding round a building, all provide patterns; so do maps aerial photographs and plans. There is pattern in almost everything we use, on the clothes we wear, and everywhere we go.

It is interesting to collect patterns from different places, to compare and contrast and to talk about why some of them seem beautiful and some so ugly.

Ideas for designs from other creative activities

It is often possible to take ideas from other activities to use in embroidery. Drawing in pencil, crayon and charcoal, and painting in tempera and oil can suggest designs, and exciting patterns can be found in leaf printing and from lino printing and potato prints. Cutting out freehand gives facility with scissors. Even blowing paint, folding wet painted paper and finger painting can give interesting designs.

Both tie and dye and batik can be enhanced with embroidery. All forms of paper collage can be used with fabric and thread to give exciting results.

Ideas can be taken from, or used with three-dimensional activities for example, clay, waste materials or pasta collage. Mosaics of all kinds are closely linked with fabric collage and patchwork.

Apart from practical activities, there is a rich variety of ideas which might be found in music, dance, poetry and story, as well as from science and mathematics.

It is essential that children at any stage are guided by the teacher to observe real life situations, to experience their own sensations and form their own ideas for picture and pattern making.

IDEAS WITH FABRIC

Collection

Collect as large a variety of fabric as possible.* Look at and feel these different fabrics. Sort them into groups and compare dull and shiny; patterned and plain; cold and warm; rough and smooth; thick and thin; transparent and opaque. Contrast the texture (or the feel). Contrast the colour (light, dark, etc). See how the fabrics react to cutting and pulling. Do they stretch? Are they transparent? Do they come to pieces easily? Not at all? How are they made?** Are they all made in the same way? What are they used for? Find as many uses as possible.

What are fabrics made from? Fabric is made from fibres; cotton, wool, silk linen, nylon, acrylic, rayon, acetate. Find out about each and where it comes from.

* Cottons, wools, knits, mixtures, nylons, damask, net of all kinds (including vegetable bags and garden net) velvets, rayons, fur, leather, suede, polythene, muslin, scrim, cheesecloth, dishcloth, lace, ribbon, braid, sacking, towelling, PVC, needlecord, silk, satin, felt, etc.

** Some fabrics are woven and can be easily frayed. (See page 30 for full details of woven fabric.)

Some fabrics are knitted and are called jersey fabrics. If you look closely through a magnifying glass, you can see that the knitted fabric looks similar to hand knitting.

Fabrics like felt and interfacings are pressed into shape and sometimes treated with heat. They do not fray or unravel.

5 String collage. Caroline (13)

Organisation

Fabric has to be kept in some sort of order either in boxes or bags. Transparent polythene sacks are good because the fabrics can be easily seen, but the dangers of polythene bags should always be borne in mind. Draw-string bags are also suitable. The bags can be stored in boxes, or on shelves, or hung on nails or hooks, or on a stand. It is up to the individual teacher to decide how fabric is sorted. Here are two suggestions. By *colour* or predominant colour,

or by *type*.

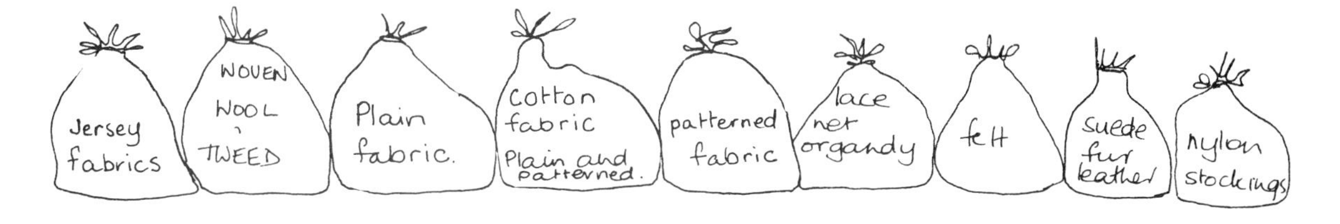

Glues

It is really well worth while finding out how these fabrics react to glue, both the strong glues which are made specially for sticking fabric, and the cellulose glues or pastes, which might be used for sticking large areas of cloth to card or paper for backgrounds, or experiments in three-dimensional work. Some fabrics dry without showing marks. Some, on the other hand change colour, or show stains. This might not matter, or the marks might fit in with the design, but if the properties of the materials are known, mistakes are not made, and time and material are saved.

Iron crumpled fabric before use.

6 Collage of fields and trees, making use of flowered fabrics for background and curtain net for clouds. Boys and girls (10–11)

Making a fabric collage picture*

A fabric collage should make use of many of the pieces of fabric in the collection and can also incorporate some of the ideas in the following pages of this first section. Each picture should be carefully discussed, before one piece of fabric is cut.** Collect the fabric to be used and iron if necessary. Now for the background,† which is just as important as the subject.

What sort of background suits the subject of the picture? Perhaps it would be better to have a plain background. Perhaps a pattern, but what sort of pattern? Striped, checked, flowery? It is sometimes impossible to find exactly the right sort of background, so a background can be constructed. Try cutting net in layers and superimposing one layer on another. Cut out flowers from other fabrics and stick these on. Cut out stripes or patterns and stick these on. Perhaps the background should be trees, or houses, or the sea or hills, or the sky. Cut out material for these and stick. Allow a background to dry before continuing. It might also need to be pressed flat with a weight of some sort.

* A collage picture is one in which all the pieces are glued down and not sewn (from the French *coller*, to stick). There are many different makes and types of glue. The one chosen should be suitable for sticking fabric, leather, cardboard, etc. It is worth trying out the glue beforehand to see how it reacts. Read the instructions carefully. Some glues are more easily managed than others, and some glues need to be left for a few minutes before sticking. Again, others need to be held for a few seconds until they hold

** Sharp scissors. A separate pair should be used for cutting paper.

† For a basis, use hessian, or furnishing fabric. Nobbly tweed and striped materials are interesting. Any non-stretch fabric may be used if it looks right. If it is very thin or transparent, line it with interlining. Sometimes it is a good idea to stick the background onto something firm like paper, card or hardboard. Stick backgrounds with cellulose (wallpaper) paste. Paste both card and back of fabric, just like wallpaper. Allow to dry thoroughly. Any additions can be stuck on in the same way.

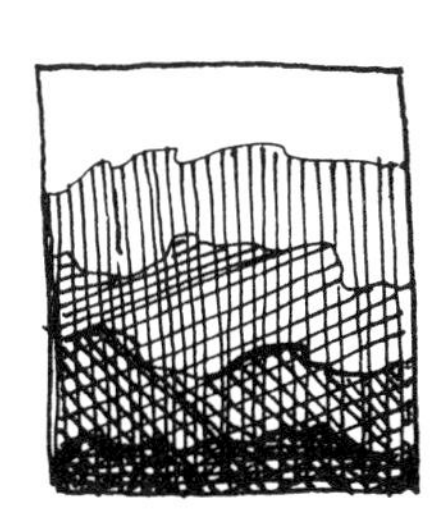
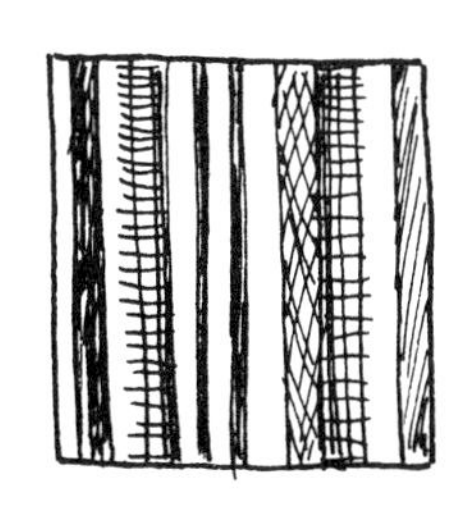

The subject of the picture is important, so try to choose fabric and colours which will contrast well with the background. Cut out the shapes freely, without using paper patterns.* Always try to find just the right fabric. Don't forget to make use of fabric which looks like buildings, hair, shoe leather, wheels, smoke, fur, jewels, windows, flower beds, etc, and try to use bits of lace, suede, leather, felt, PVC and even bits of silver foil. Think of colour. Would the picture be better in light tones, or in dark colours? Should it be made in tones of one colour or in contrasting colours. Sometimes it is worth making a picture in dark tones to see the effect.

* As pictures became more complicated, it may be necessary to make and use a template. However, practise in cutting simple shapes freehand, gives confidence in handling scissors and in using the eye.

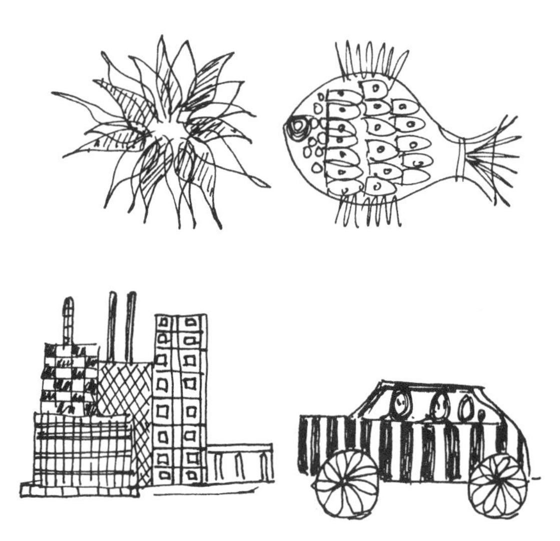

Perhaps it would be interesting to use only black and white. What about texture? Is the subject hairy, furry, smooth, nobbly, leathery, silky, rough, ribbed? Is there any suitable fabric? Make the materials work for you. It is a good idea to arrange most of the picture before gluing.** When the subject looks satisfactory glue firmly. Have a good look at it. Is it too empty? Would it look better with more decoration?

** See previous page. To apply glue, it is sometimes better to use something more delicate than the applicator provided. Try a carpet needle, or a cocktail stick. Practise using as little glue as possible. A thick blob of glue can spoil a picture.

Sometimes a fabric picture can look rather flat. Here are some suggestions for giving a three-dimensional effect. The ideas are set out as separate exercises, but if a fabric picture is being constructed, any or all can be used in decorating one picture, and any shape can be used. Choose thick material like felt, leather, carpet felt, blanket, tweed, suede, etc. Cut out the shapes* in different sizes. Build these up on top of each other (like bricks) with the biggest at the bottom, to make a three dimensional pattern. Stick** onto a background.† When using glue, always work on a flat surface, and not on a wall or an easel. The glue should have plenty of time to set before the picture is hung on the wall.

* Circles, squares, triangles. Use uneven shapes, too.

** Use a strong fabric glue. Follow the instructions on the label.

† Backgrounds for three dimensional work should be rigid. Fabric can be pasted or glued onto card, paper or hardboard.

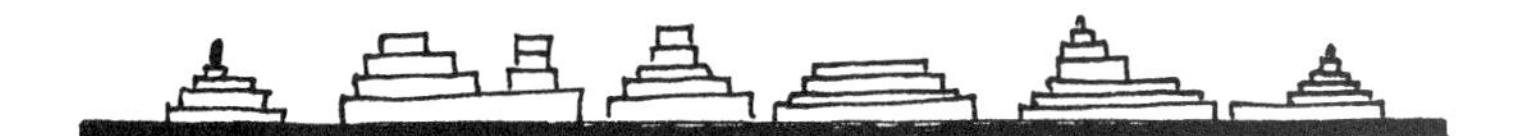

Cross-section showing layers of fabric

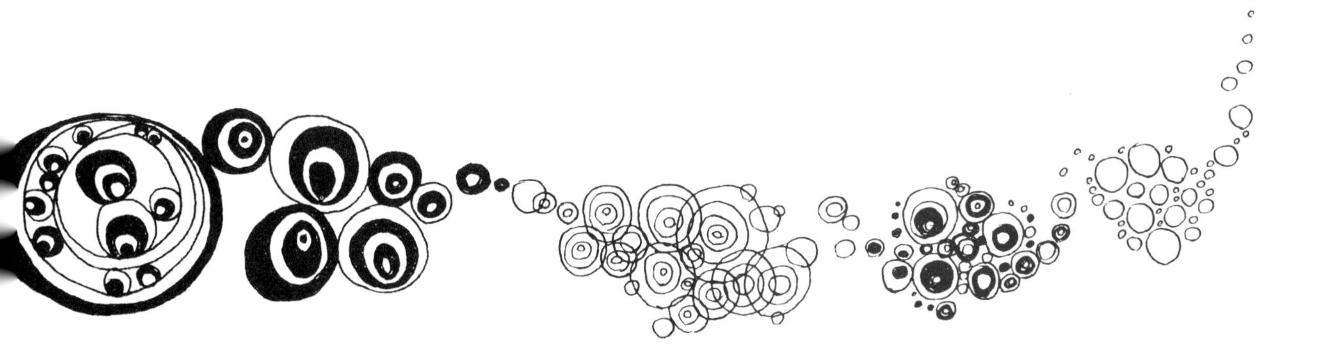

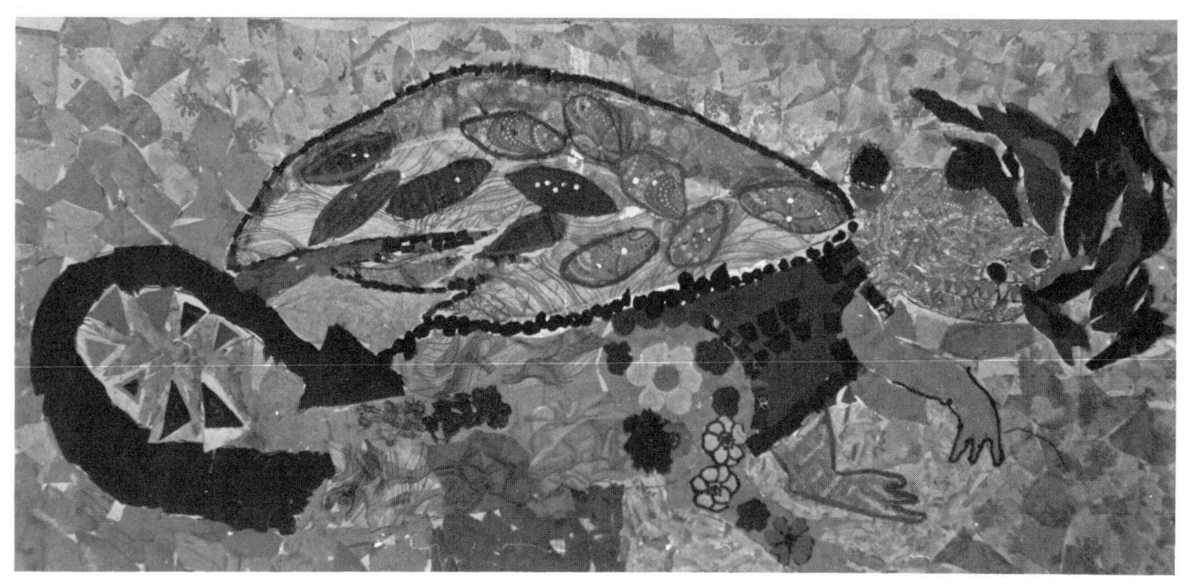

7 Collage of dragon. Different fabric shapes have been built up on the background and on the dragon itself, sometimes in layers, sometimes in groups. Boys and girls (7–8)

8 Embroidered dragon.

Using strips of fabric

Cut a strip of fabric. Glue one end and roll into a tight tube.* Cut different lengths and widths of material so that the tubes are all different sizes, thin, thick, tall and short. When the tubes are stuck, arrange them on the background.** Stick them down as if they were growing out of the background. Try wool and tweed, felt, leather, suede, striped fabric, corduroy.

* Hold for a moment until stuck. Or tie a piece of thread round or a rubber band to hold securely until firm.

** Fabric on paper, card, or hardboard.

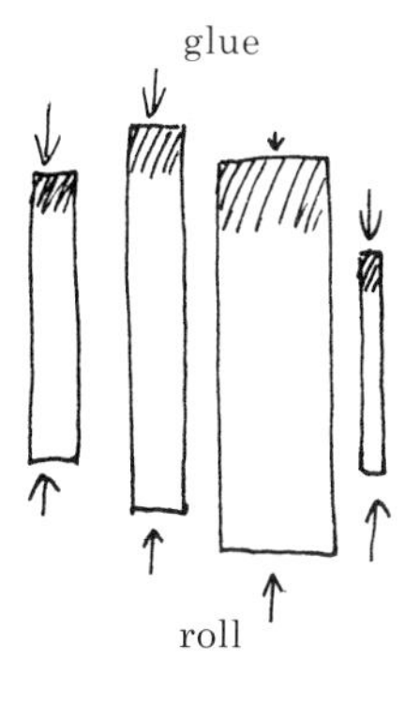

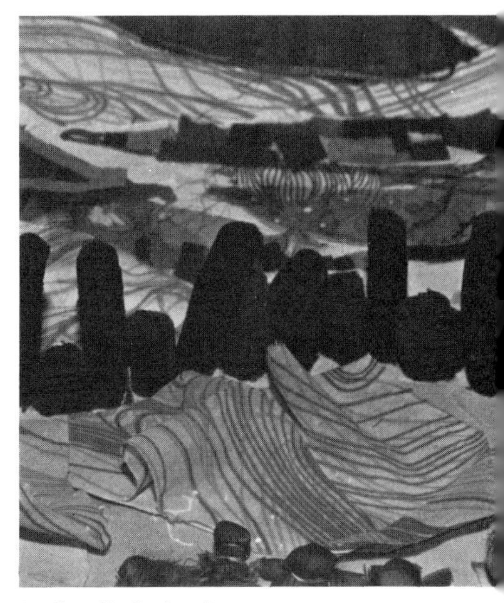

9 Detail of tube shapes

An interesting variation of this is to fringe the edge of the strips of material, by taking out some of the edge threads. Try to cut the material on the weft and warp, so that the fringe is even.

Woollen tweed and hessian are very good for this, and easy to fray.

Roll the material as above and stick down onto the background material. The fringes stick up like shaving brushes. Vary the length of the fringe as well as the height of the tubes.

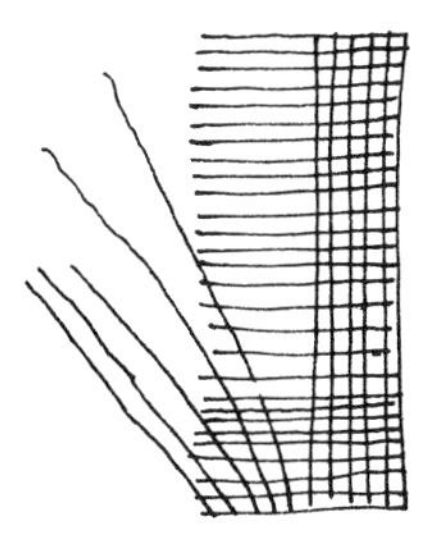

10 Detail of dragon on facing page

It is also possible to cut strips of material as before, but instead of rolling tightly, glue the end over the other end to leave a hole in the middle like a hoop or tube.

These tubes can be stuck down on their sides, in rows or at angles to each other. If the material used is strong, it is possible to put them in heaps,* and to put one inside another.

The tubes can also be stuck down end up, like chimney pots. Try putting one inside another.

* This is more difficult and needs practice.

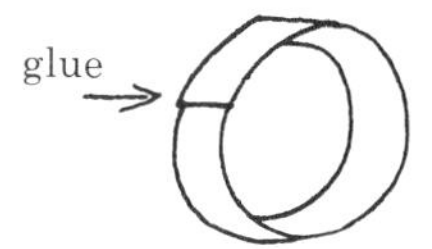

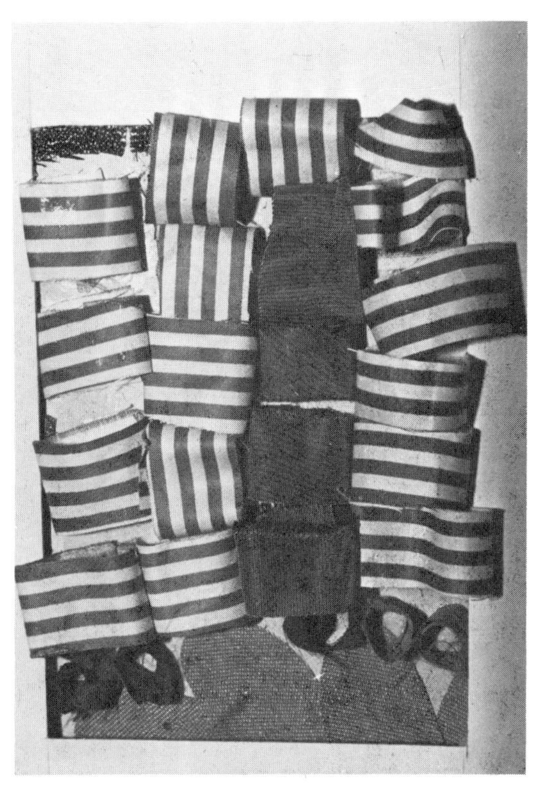

11 Loops horizontal and vertical. Note use of striped fabric

An interesting effect can be achieved by making arches from strips of material. Cut strips of fabric* in different lengths and various widths, and glue at each end.

* Try various fabrics to see which is most effective. Stiffer fabrics stand up well. Try also corduroy strips, strips of jersey fabric, strips of tights.

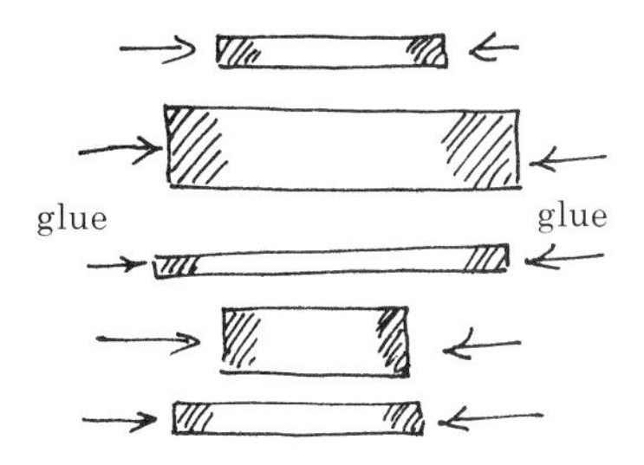

Stick onto background in arches. Place in lines, or at angles to each other. Place big arches over small arches. Try different fabrics.

Use all the same colour or use contrasting colours.

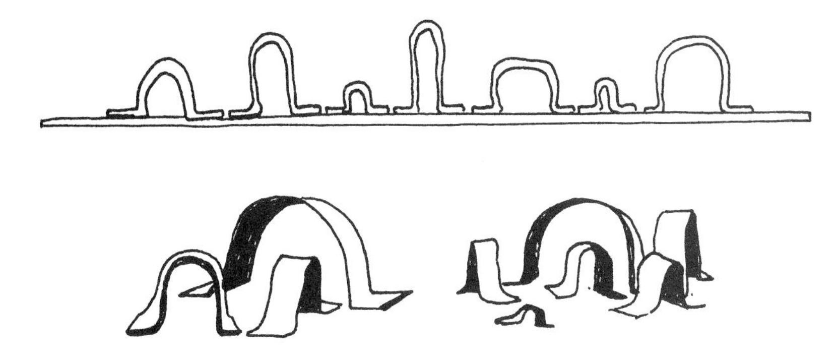

Another idea is to cut a circle (freehand) then to cut a spiral out of the circle. Stick the outside end of the spiral onto the background. Pick out the centre of the spiral. Pull it out and stick onto the background. This makes a sort of curl. Try groups of these using different materials and different sizes.

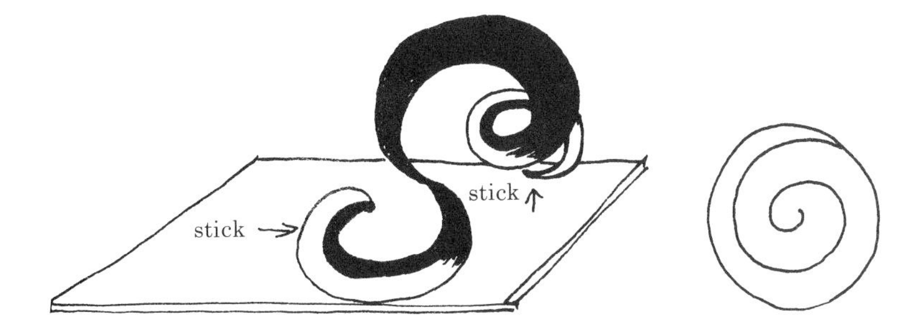

Three-dimensional work

To give flat shapes a more three dimensional quality, cardboard or polystyrene shapes can be used as a base and covered with fabric. There are several ways of doing this depending on the shape and the material used.

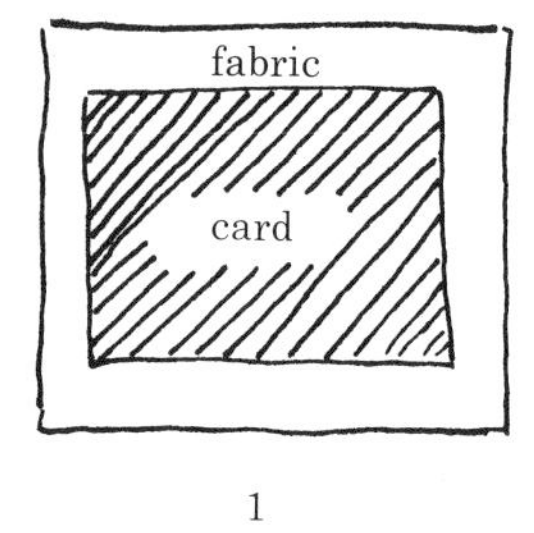

1

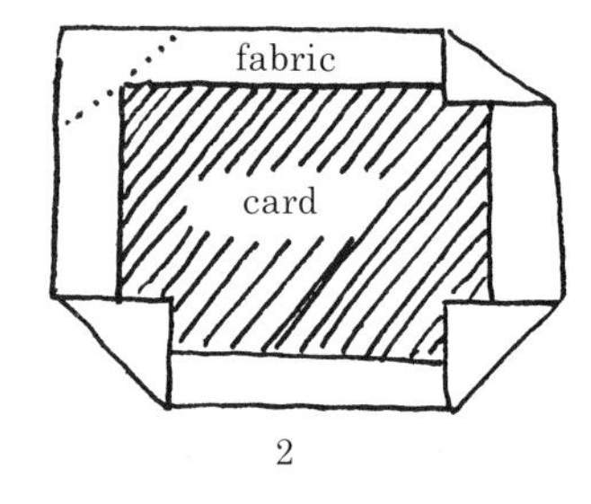

2

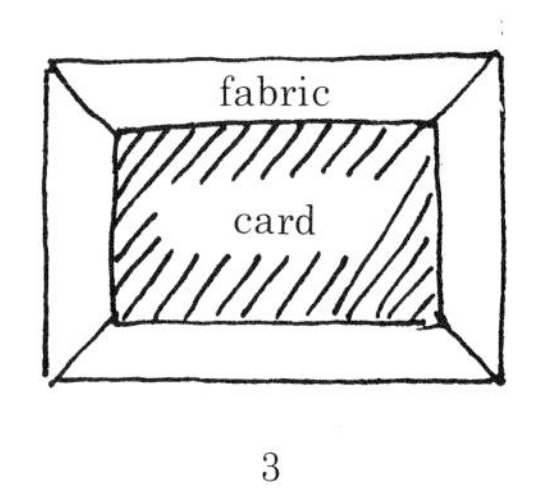

3

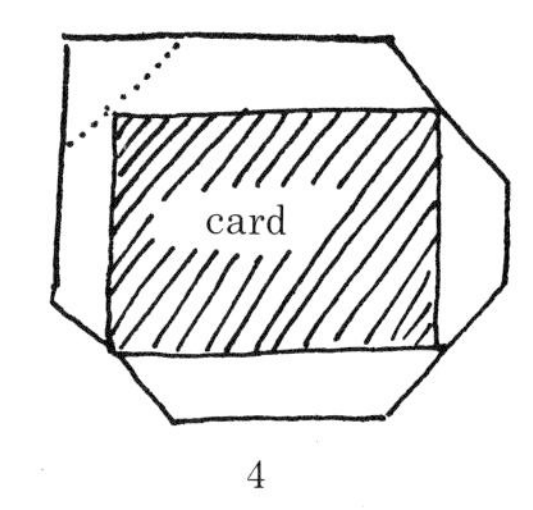

4

To cover a rectangular shape

1 Cut a rectangle of fabric about 1 cm bigger than the card shape.

2 Glue the corners of the fabric and fold onto the card.

3 Glue all the remaining fabric showing round the card and fold over onto the card. Hold to dry. Try to make the corners as sharp as possible by pulling the fabric right up to the edge of the card. If the material used for covering the card is very thick,* it is sometimes better to cut the corners right off.

4 Glue the sides and fold in as in 3. Hold to stick.

* Like tweed, blanket, etc.

To cover a circle or irregular shape

1 Cut fabric 1 cm larger than shape.

2 Make cuts into the fabric just to the edge of the card.

3 Glue fabric which shows round the edge of the card. Press cut pieces onto card. Hold to stick. Pull material right up against card for a good shape. These shapes can be overlapped, or built up.

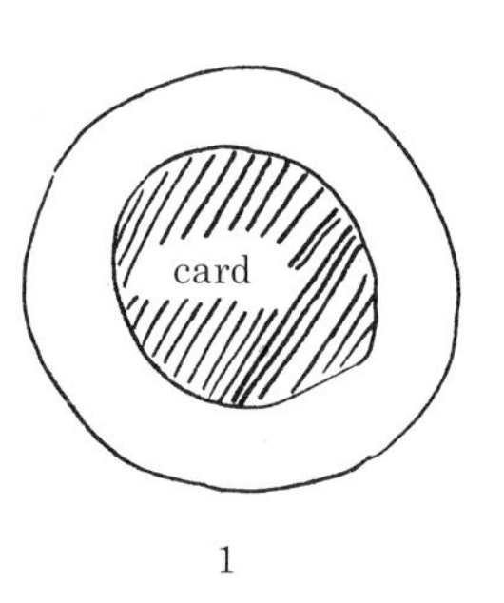

1

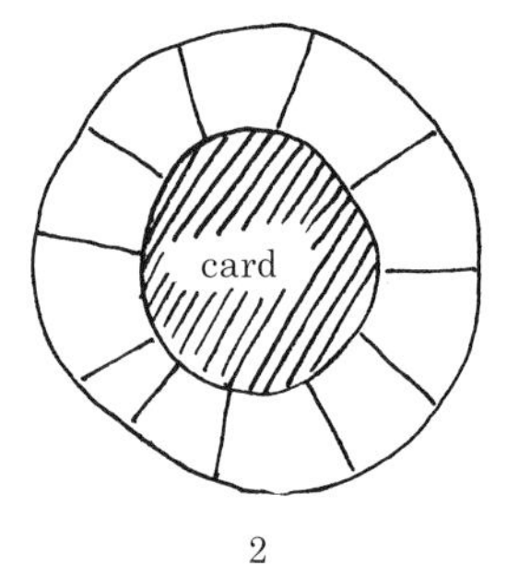

2

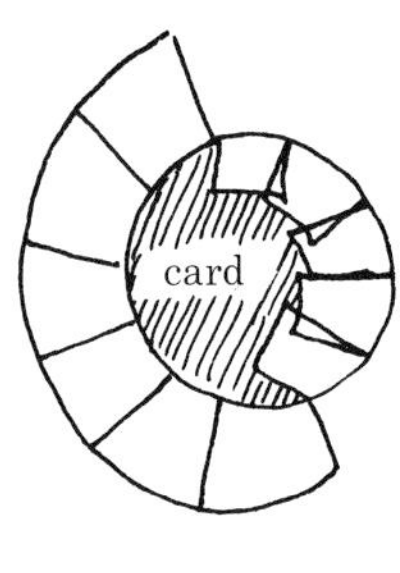

3

To cover a long thin strip of card or wood, a tube,* a circle or a rounded shape with a hole in the middle, cut a long strip of fabric. Attach one end to the shape with glue. Bind the shape gradually by winding the strip of fabric round and round the shape. Overlap the fabric onto itself so that the card does not show.

When using a fine fabric like rayon, taffeta or cotton polyester, it is easier to dip the whole strip in cellulose paste** so that it is soaked, and then wind it round the shape. Leave to dry thoroughly.

* Cardboard tubes are good bases for this. Insides of kitchen and toilet rolls.

** Wallpaper paste.

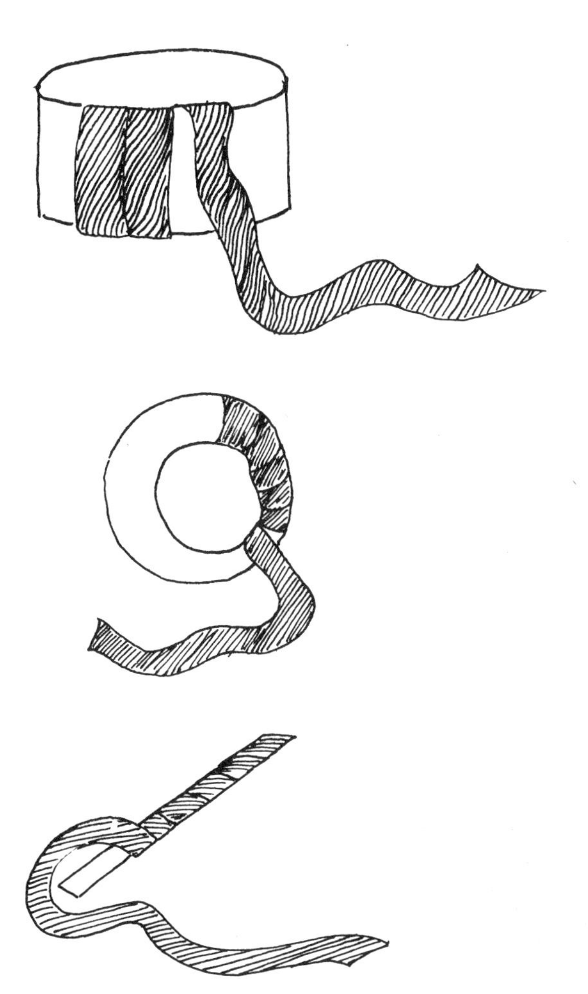

It is possible to build up card and polystyrene shapes in relief on a firm base, then completely to cover the whole structure with thin fabric soaked in cellulose paste. Papier mâché and wire shapes can also be covered in the same way. Experiment as much as possible.

Transparent materials

* Any sort of transparent material, including nets of all kinds; organdie, nylon, lace, polythene, chiffon, tulle, plastic net.

** Include light net over dark material and vice versa. Look at patterns and dull, shiny and plain fabrics. Also look at transparent fabric over tissue paper, tinfoil, sweet wrappers, doylies.

† Run a little glue round the edge of the shape with a cocktail stick or a large needle. Use a strong glue.

Look at different transparent fabrics.*Try to decide why they are transparent. Are they holey? Are they made of fine material? Are they loosely woven? The idea of working with these materials is to exploit the transparency. Therefore look at as many different backgrounds** as possible through each transparent fabric. How are they different from each other and which is most effective?

Now, cut out groups of transparent shapes in different sizes. Find a suitable background and arrange the shapes on this. When they are arranged satisfactorily, stick† them on. Also try groups of shapes in different materials, but including transparent fabrics. Cut holes in some shapes. Try using all the same colour. Try all black and all white. Try sticking sequins behind the nets.

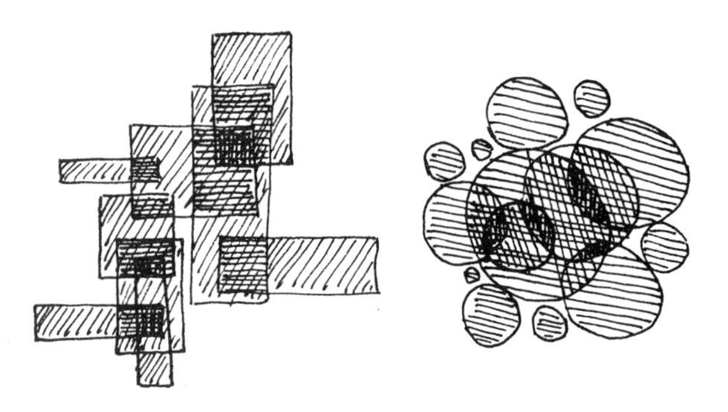

Some materials, including organdie and net, are quite stiff. If only one edge or point of the cut out shape is glued to the background, the shape will stand away by itself. If several shapes are glued close together, with some shapes overlapping others, quite a three dimensional effect can be achieved.

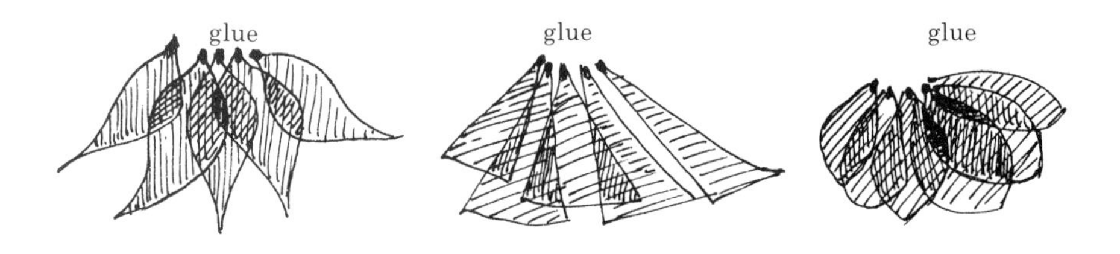

Some of the softer transparent fabrics can be soaked in cellulose* paste, then stuck onto a background. First, try cutting strips of transparent fabric and sticking them onto a background. Superimpose some. This is a good way of making the background for a collage picture (see page 15).

* Tulle, chiffon, nylon (lingerie fabric), net if it is soft. New nylon net is rather harsh and unmanageable, but can be boiled in detergent, which does soften it a little.

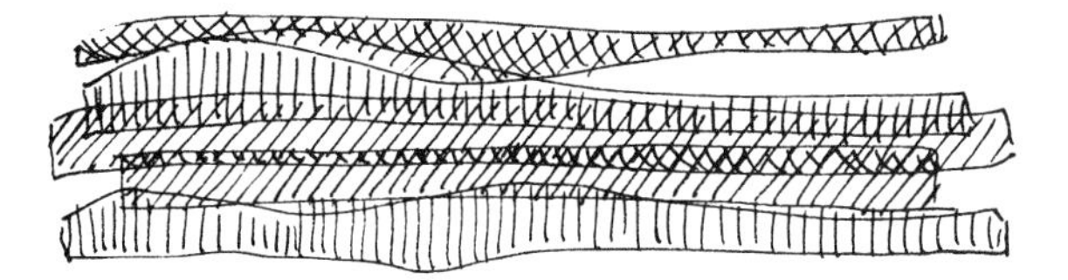

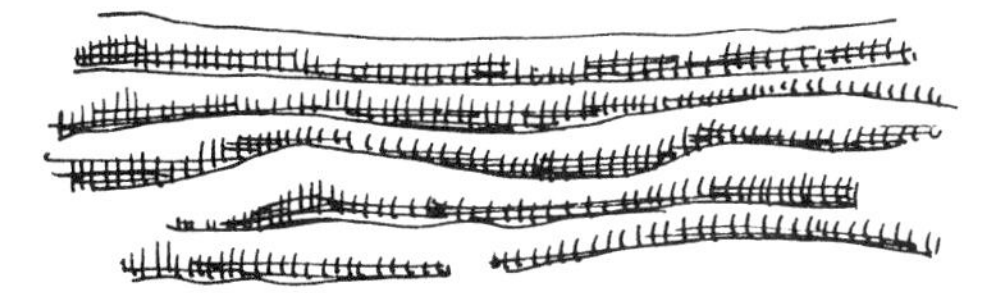

Use different colours, or just one colour. The soaked fabric can also be pleated onto the background. Press the fabric to the background between the pleats and round the edge with the fingers. Add more paste if necessary. A piece of soaked transparent fabric can be pushed around into hills and valleys with the fingers or with a stick, making swirls and gathers in the material. These have to be left to dry completely when they are finished. The middle cannot be pressed under a weight to flatten as this would spoil the effect, but try to flatten the edges where the material and background meet. If, when dry, the material round the edge lifts, glue it down with strong glue.

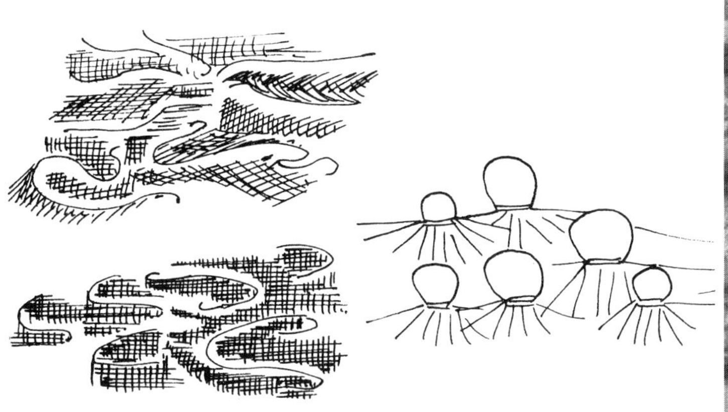

11a Detail of stuffed shapes

Quite an interesting effect can be achieved with transparent fabric,** by taking up a small piece of the material and putting into it a piece of coloured wool or fabric, or even silver paper. Put a small rubber band, or tie a piece of thread tightly round the neck of the bundle to hold it in. This makes little knobs all over the fabric and the material pleats in between.

** Nylon fabrics, organdie, tulle and chiffon are best for this.

Geometric shapes

Make patterns from geometric shapes such as circles or squares, etc. Build up linear patterns (or borders). Start with a simple shape. Arrange the shapes in a line. Add some more shapes and embellish again, and again.

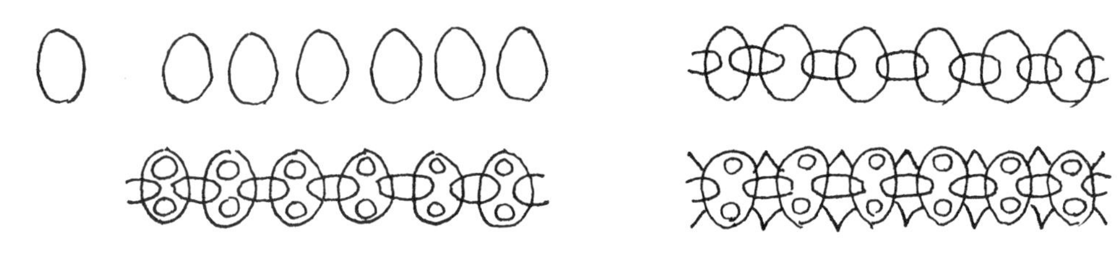

Make a collection of linear patterns from the environment. Fences and walls, even barbed wire; patterns on a wall, on a carpet, on a blind. Patterns from India and Egypt, Constantinople and Greece.

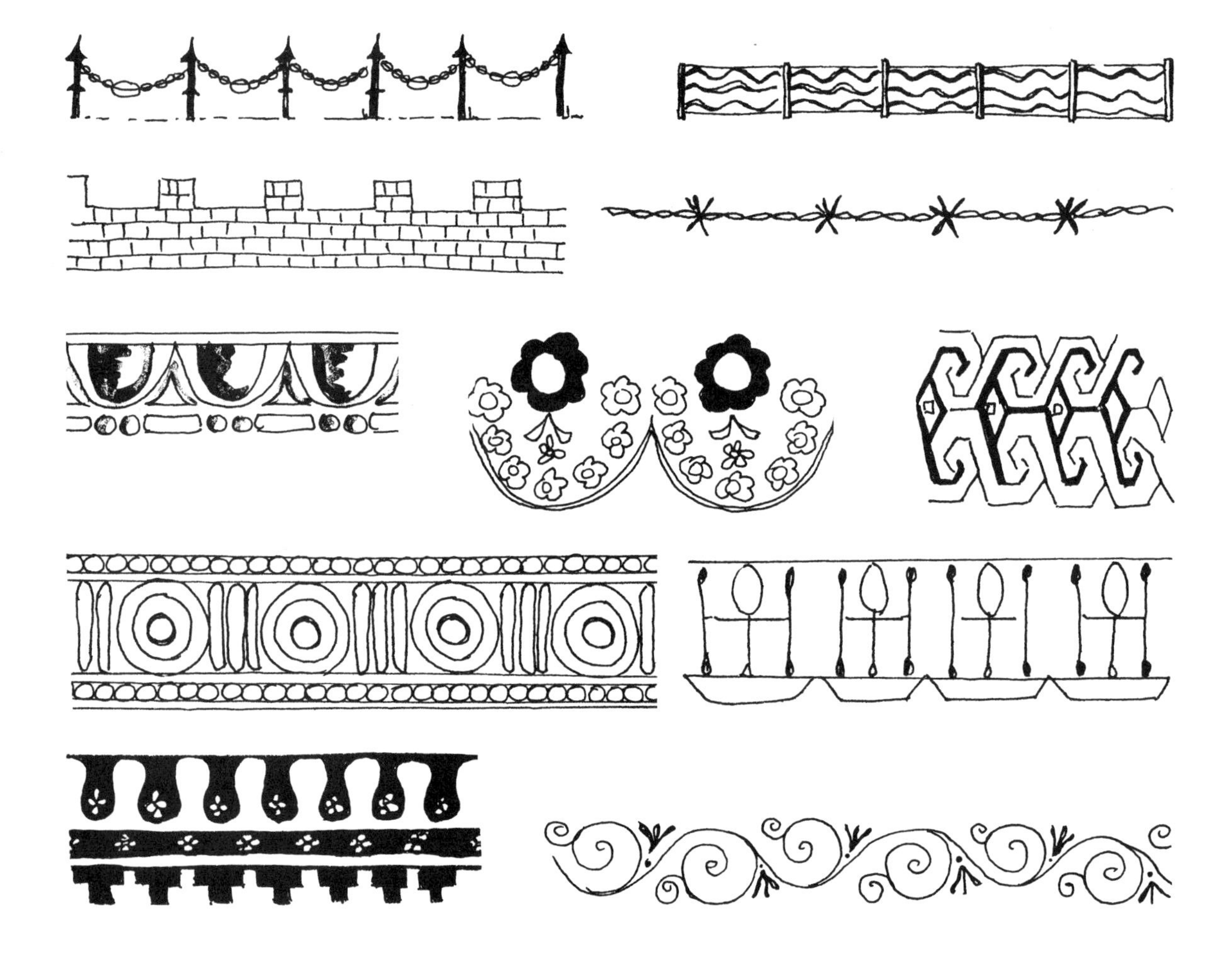

Build up block patterns. Start with a simple pattern in a square. Repeat it in blocks. Try several different patterns.

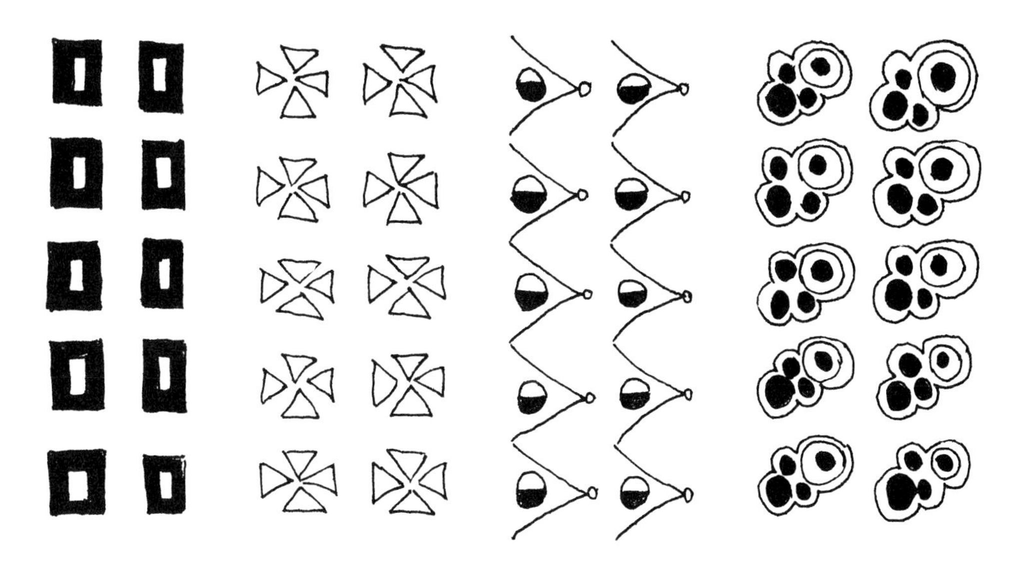

Make patterns with stencils. Cut stencil in paper or card.

Use paint and paper. Use fabric paint and cloth. Use potato or carrot prints. Use a knife to cut the pattern. Stick string patterns onto blocks of wood, to make string prints.

Potato prints
(or carrots)
Use a knife

String prints
Stick string pattern onto wood block

IDEAS WITH FABRIC

* Circles, rectangles, triangles, etc. Large and small. Try different triangle shapes and different rectangle shapes. Try other geometric shapes.

Using any fabric, cut out shapes* in different sizes. Arrange pieces side by side in a linear pattern. Arrange also in blocks of pattern.

Now try to cut shapes all the same without using a ruler or pencil. Arrange in a linear pattern.

Now arrange shapes in blocks.

Next, cut shapes from striped fabric. Make the stripes go in different directions.

Mix patterned and plain material, light and dark material. See the effect of one colour in two tones.

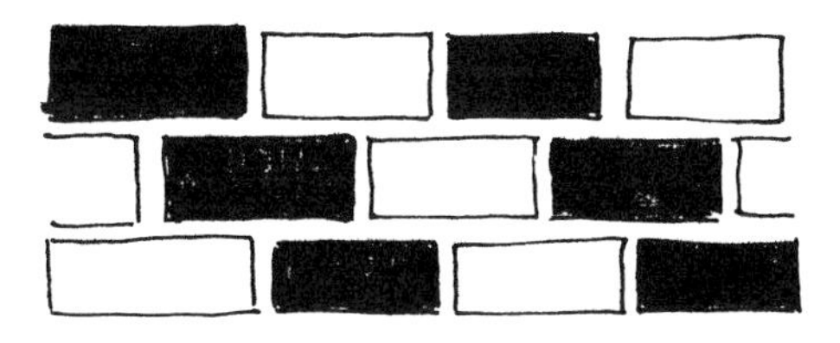

Use shiny and dull fabric. Use stripes with spots and checks with flowered fabric. When a pleasing pattern has been found, stick the pieces onto a background. Compare the patterns. See how different they are. Make a collection.

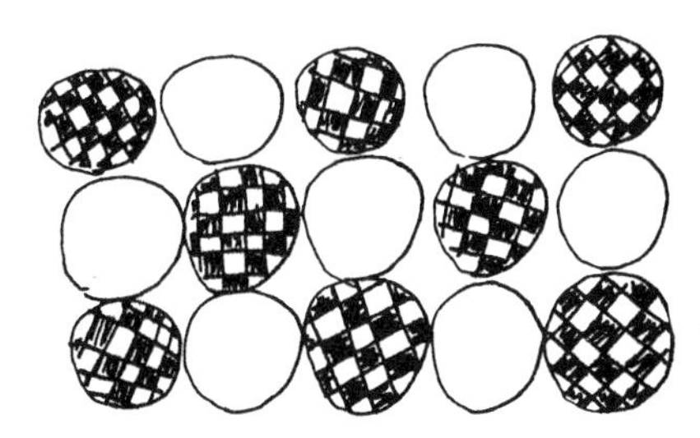

Woven fabric

* Find material woven from different fibres like wool, cotton, rayon, nylon, linen.

Black threads are warps.

White threads are wefts.

Choose some fabric which is woven* to see how it is made. If you look closely, you can see that threads have been woven under and over each other, rather like a basket, to hold them together, to make the piece of cloth. Sometimes the weaves are slightly more complicated, eg the weft might pass over more than one warp, but the general principal of weaving is the same. Try looking at a piece of woven cloth under a magnifying glass. Pull apart a small piece to see how it is made. The threads parallel to the selvage are the warp threads. The threads going across are the weft. It is difficult to see this on a small piece of fabric, but on a roll of material in a shop, the warp goes right along the whole length of the fabric, and the weft threads go across.

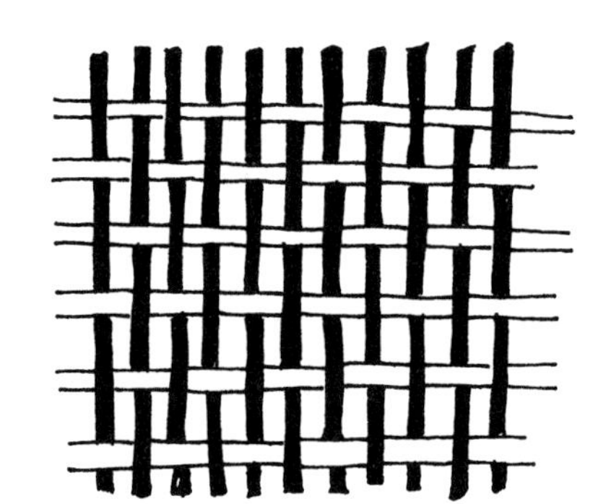

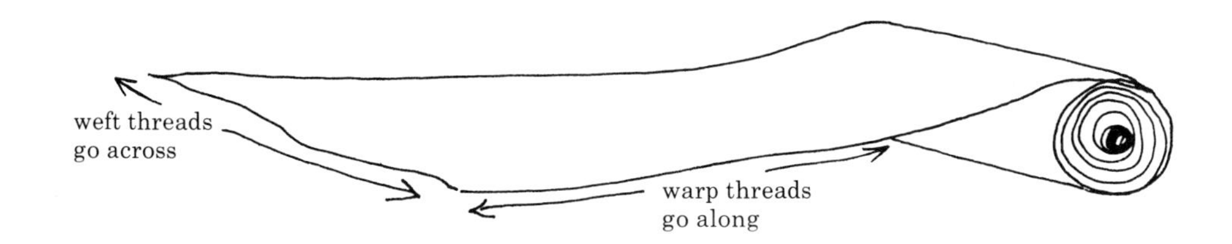

Cut a piece of material along the weft and warp to make a rectangle.

Pull it up and down. Across. Diagonally. Which pulls most, and which stretches least?

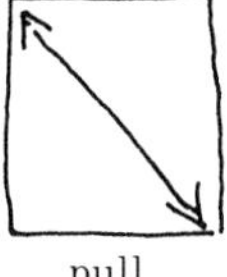
pull

pull

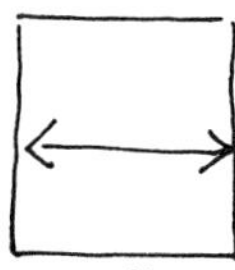
pull

12–17 Experiments with fabric shapes. Girls (12–14)

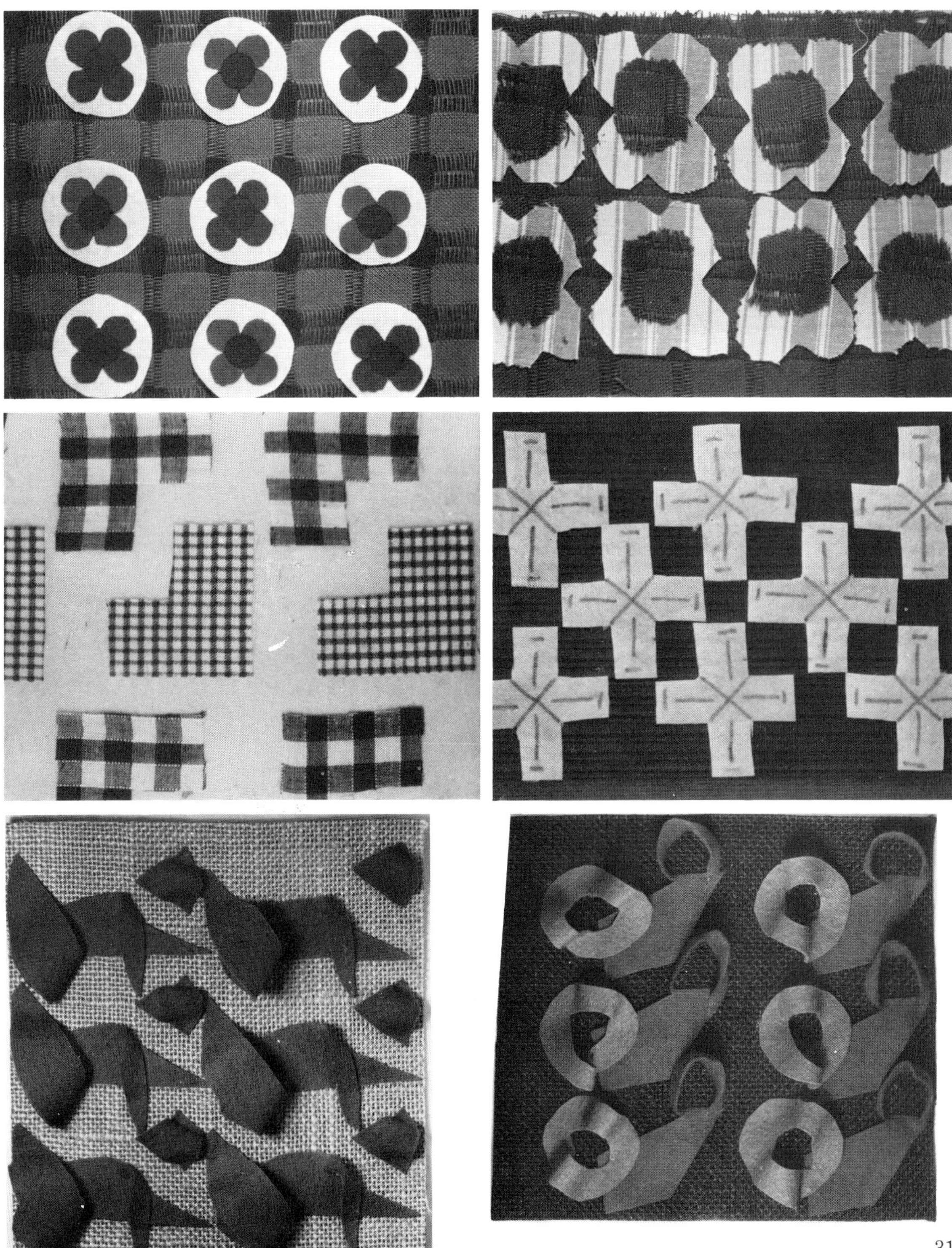

Because woven material stretches diagonally, it is a good idea to cut fabric patterns so that the warps run down and the weft runs across the material, even in uneven shapes like this.

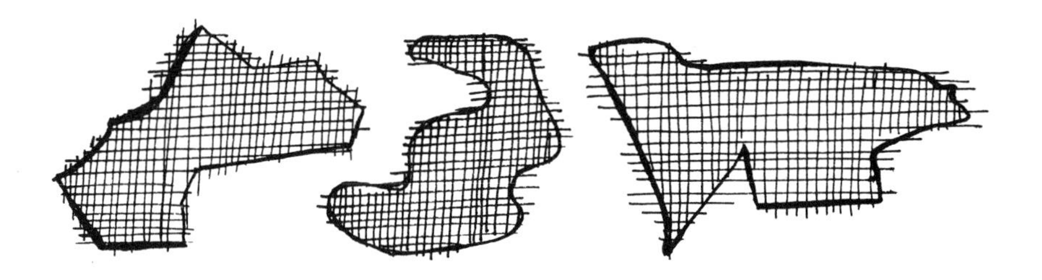

Now try cutting patterns and blocks of patterns so that the weft and warp run across and down. If the fabric has a stripe, check or regular pattern, this can sometimes help.

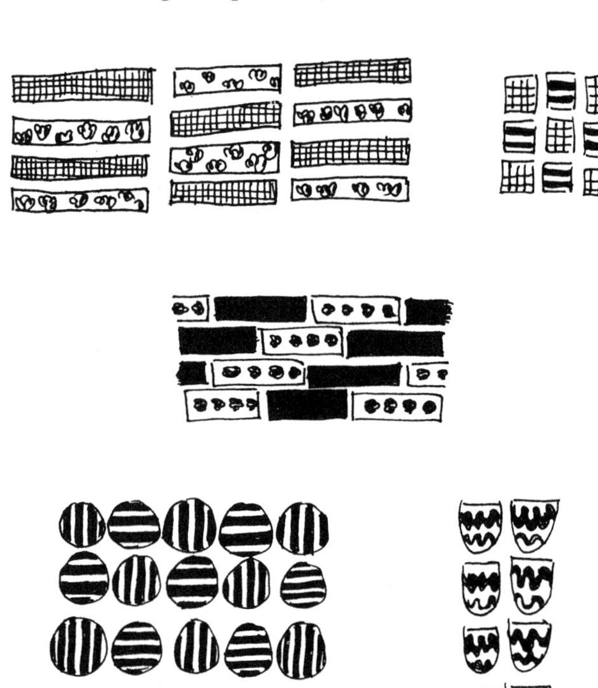

Try different colours and patterns together. See which one looks the most attractive. Stick material onto a background. Make patterns with the same fabric type, eg all tweed, all cotton, all velvet, all corduroy, all rayon.

IDEAS WITH THREAD

Collection

Thread and yarn* can be wound onto rolls of paper, empty toilet rolls, a cross of card, and empty cotton reels, unless they are already wound on cones or in neat balls. Store in shallow boxes, so that the types can easily be seen. Have a couple of people in charge to keep the threads wound and tidy. Include threads unravelled from other fabrics, particularly tweeds, which have very interesting threads.

* Including cottons of all kinds, embroidery silks, tapestry wool, carpet wool, knitting yarns of all kinds and all thicknesses, weaving yarns, metallic thread, string, raffia, raffene, ric-rac braid and other braids, ribbon.

Children can also make threads from various things which can first be dyed.

Dyeing
Use a large pan on the stove to dye small bundles of thread or fabric. It is also possible to dye larger amounts very successfully in the washing machine. The instructions can be found on the tins and bottles of dye which are available. Try dyeing** some of the following. The light colours will dye most true, but the darker colours will take on the tone of the other materials. Pieces of net, lace, ribbon, nylon underslips, tights, string and metallic yarn, corduroy, ric-rac braid. Experiment with different yarns and fabrics.

Rinse and spread the finished pieces on newspaper to dry. Iron while still damp.

** When dyeing string or yarn, wind into a hank and tie securely with a piece of strong cotton, or the yarns will become inextricably entangled.

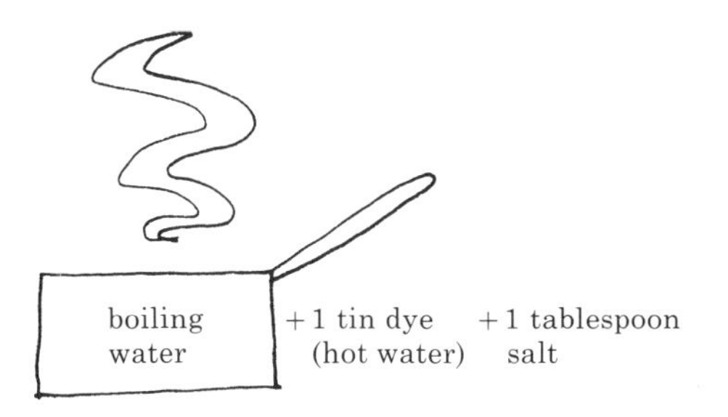

18–19 Use of various threads and strips of fabric for weaving. Including weaving yarns, raffia, lace, fur fabric, cotton, wool, strips of woven and non-woven fabric. Also pipe cleaners, straws, beads and strips of wood. Erica and Nichola (10) (left). Kathryn (10) (right)

Making threads

To make threads from corduroy, simply cut along the channels on the material. Make some wide and some narrow strips. Try to find both thick and fine corduroy.

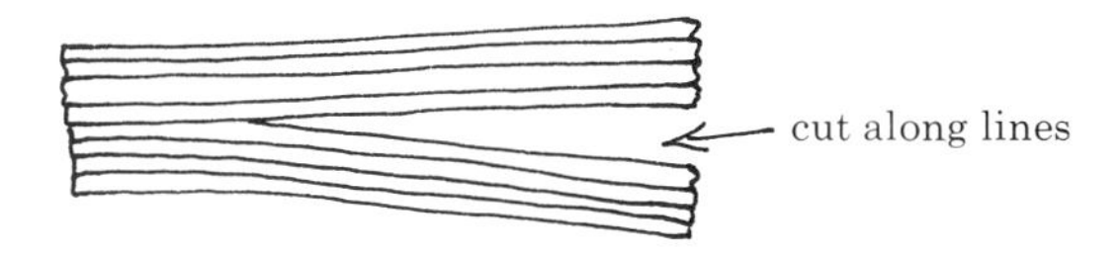

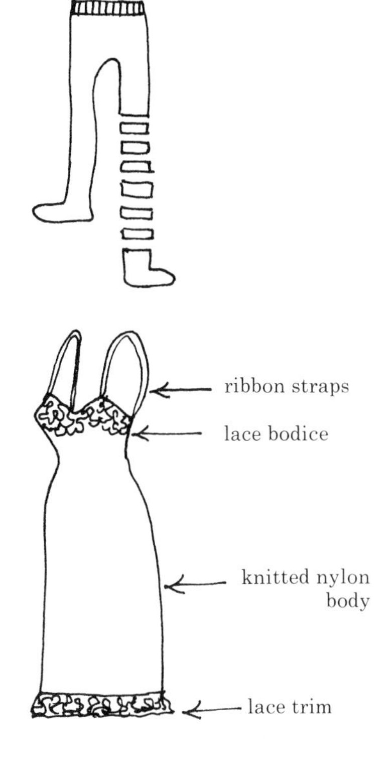

Tights are very useful, and dye beautifully. Cut across leg and resulting circle to make one thread. Pull and the material will form a roll. This is strong and can be used both for weaving and sometimes for sewing.

Nylon underslips are made from fabric which, when cut into strips, rolls into a thread which can be used in weaving. The ribbons and lace can also be used in weaving.

Other fabrics will sometimes make satisfactory threads when cut into strands. Try net, PVC, leather, suede and also jersey fabrics, which do not fray.

Some threads have little knobs at intervals. These are called *slubs* and give the yarn an interesting texture. Slubbed yarns are used in weaving. It is possible to make slubbed threads by tying knots at intervals, along a piece of wool, string or cotton.

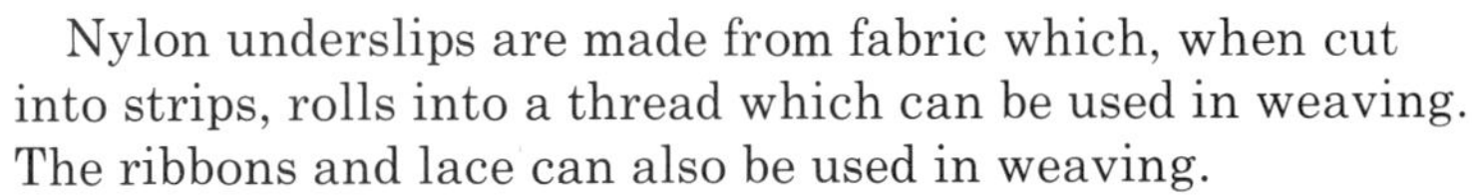

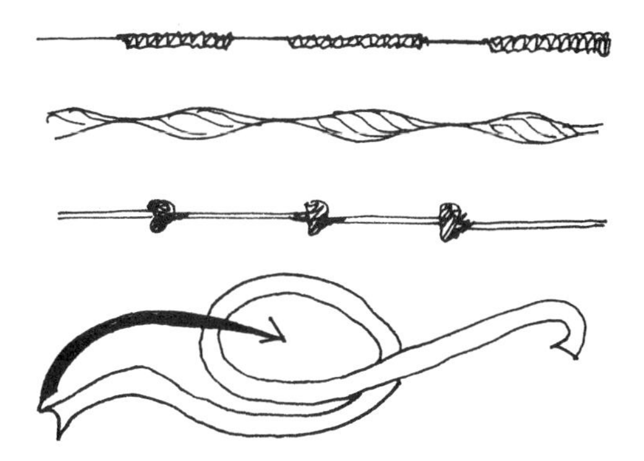

20–23 First experiments in weaving
20 Fabric covered card. Helen (10)
21 Circle bound with fabric. Huw (10)
22 Fabric covered polystyrene meat tray. Erica (10)
23 Simple card weaving, hung on a branch. Christopher (10)

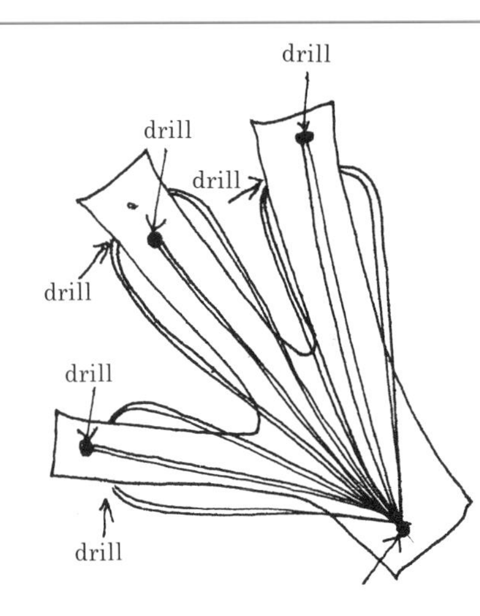

(Right)
A piece of driftwood used as a loom
Drill a hole through base, and two through each branch.
Thread warps through holes

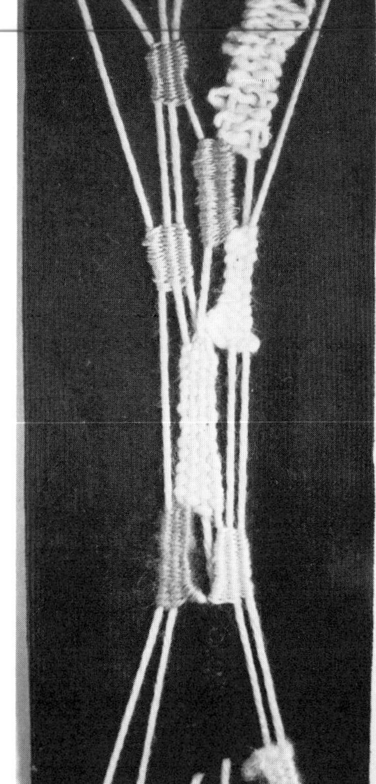

Making shapes for weaving

It is interesting to wind threads round strong card or polystyrene shapes.* Now these threads can be used as a basis for weaving and act as warps.

Preparing a card loom.

Use strong thread** and tie firmly. An odd number of warps is easier to tie at the back.

* Polystyrene and card shapes, vegetable trays from the supermarket.

** String, carpet, thread, plastic string, even fisherman's line. It must be strong and it must be secured tightly as it is under tension.

Polystyrene shapes should be covered with fabric, as they break easily.

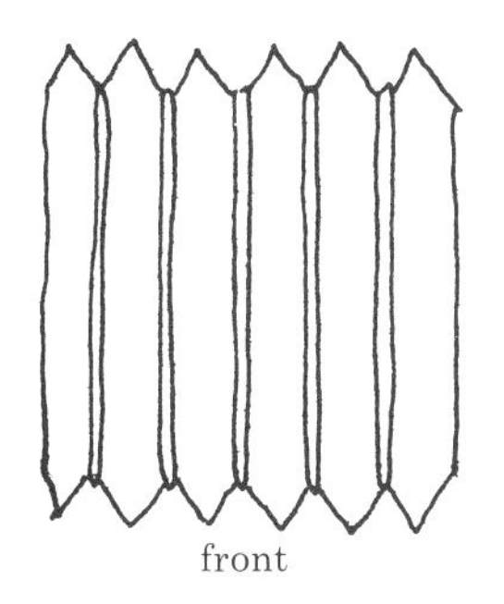

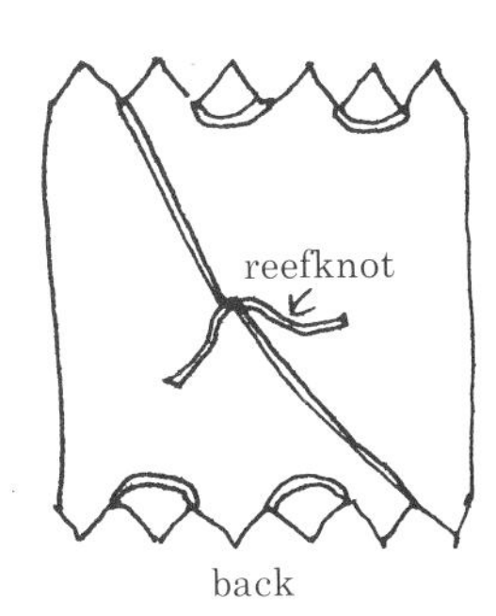

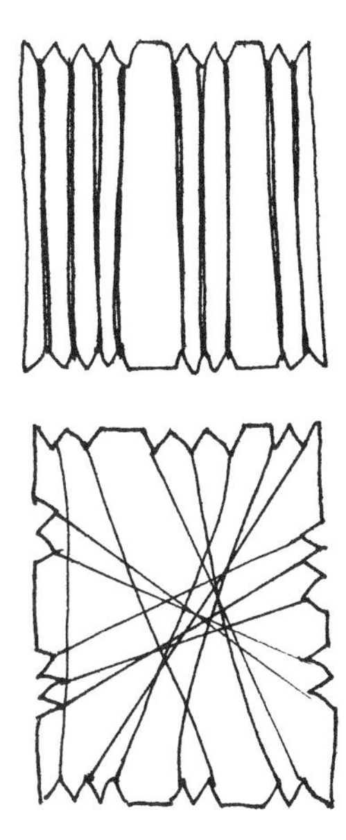

A round loom needs an odd number of warps. Start first from centre.

Shapes can be covered with a suitable material before attaching the warps. Round shapes can be covered with a strip of material wound round and round and stuck or sewn at the back. An embroidery hoop or a large hoop can be covered in this way, or a small ring can be made with card or polystyrene.

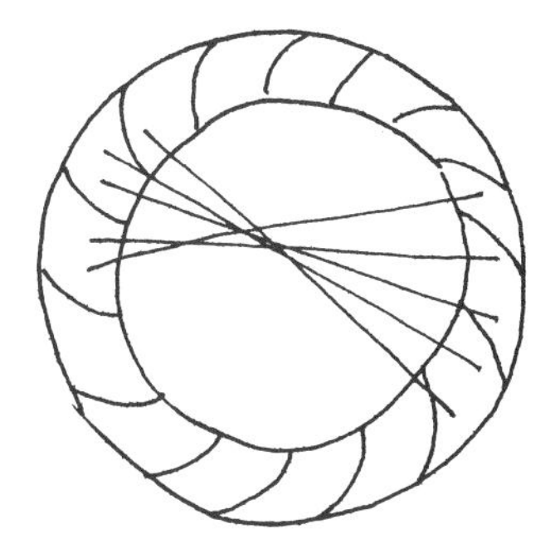

Thread a few warps, weave, then thread a few more warps and weave these, to avoid a muddle where the warps cross.

A square shape with a hole in the middle can be covered in material. Do this once at each side to cover both sides. Warps are then threaded through material and across the hole. Again thread only a few warps, then weave, and repeat, to avoid a mess where the warps cross.

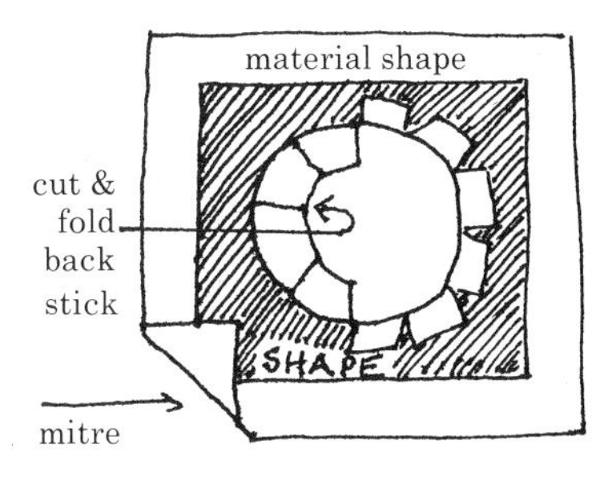

Weaving thread

Try different threads for weaving, to see how each reacts. Some look better than others. Even sewing cotton can be used. Use a large blunt needle with an eye which can easily be threaded, or a weaving needle.

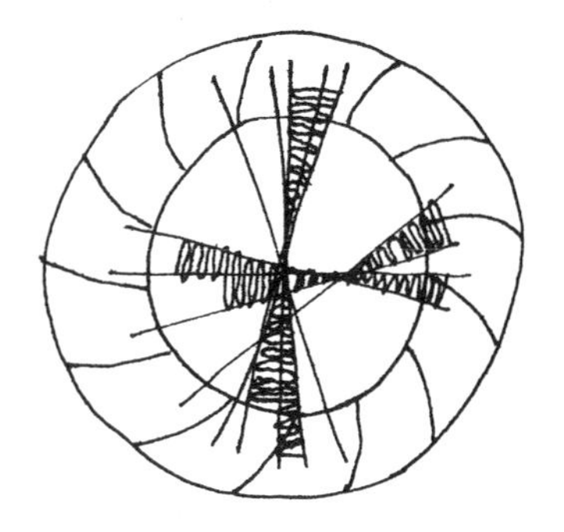

How to weave
The weft thread goes under and over the warp threads. On the return journey, the weft goes under where it went over before, and so on. It is possible to weave over two warps only. Where one warp occurs, twist the weft thread round and round. Experiment with free weaving. It is not necessary to weave over all the warps in this sort of weaving. Experiment on different shapes and use a variety of threads.

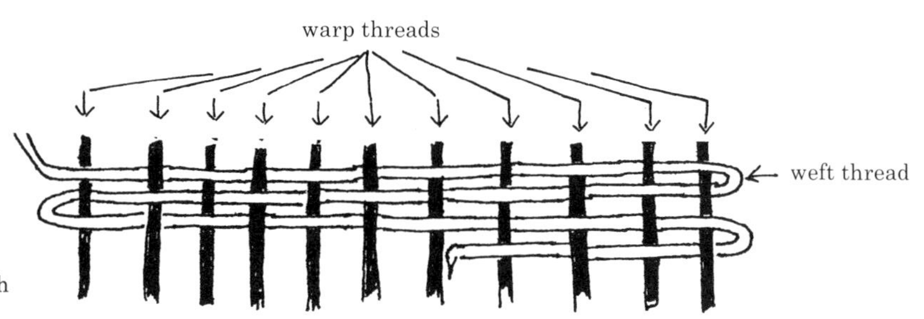

Practise weaving technique with paper strips.

24 Variation on weaving with paper strips. Paula (10)

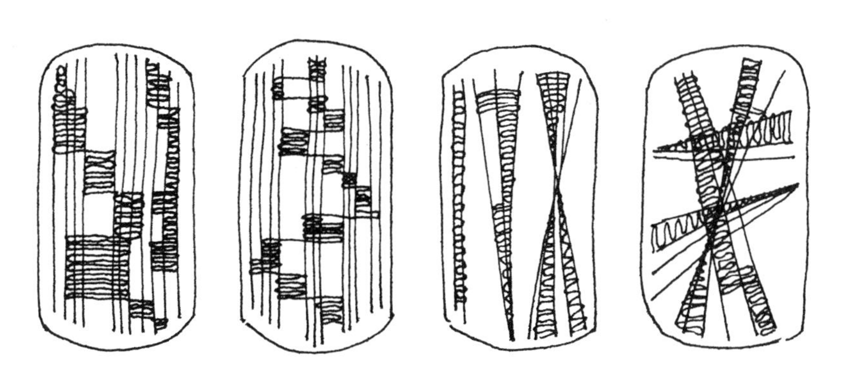

To finish off
Weave the thread back through the work already done. Cut thread. To start off a new thread carefully slide up through the work already done with a needle and thread to the starting point.

Making a loom

It is possible to make a small loom from two pieces of wood (about 2 cm × 4 cm and 30 cm long) joined with another piece of wood nailed or screwed into place. Nails or hardboard pins are knocked into the two parallel pieces, exactly opposite each other, about 1 cm apart. Starting from one corner, the warps are wound round the nails, keeping the warps taut. Use very strong thread or string. Finish off securely.*

* To finish off, do a half hitch like this, two or three times.

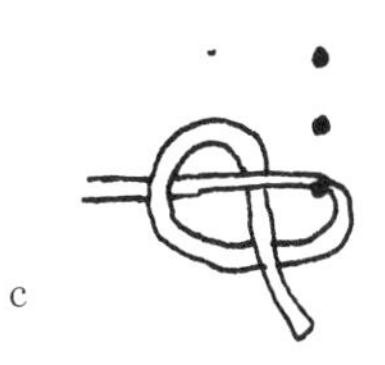

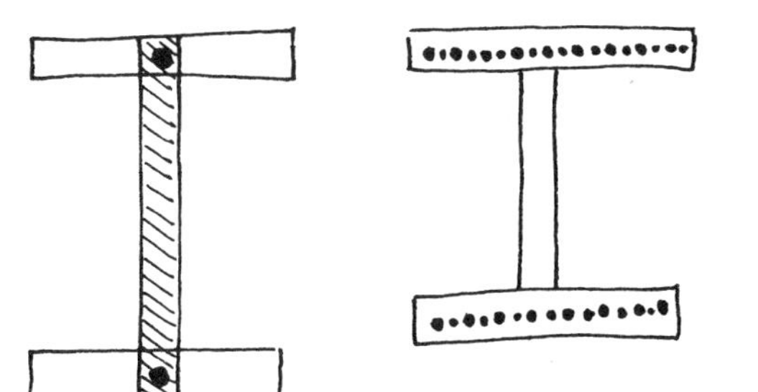

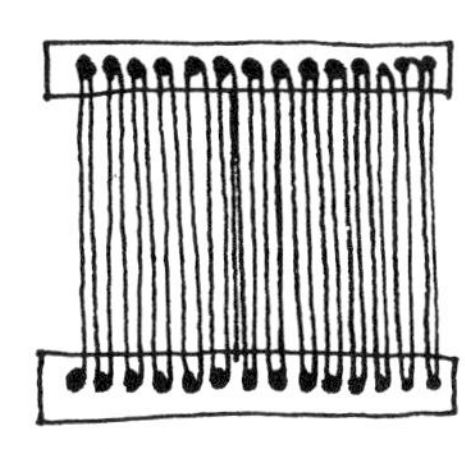

Now the weaving can be started. Try out unusual threads, and 'made' threads.** Long threads can be wound round a cardboard shuttle which will keep them tidy and untangled.

** Threads made from other materials see page 35.

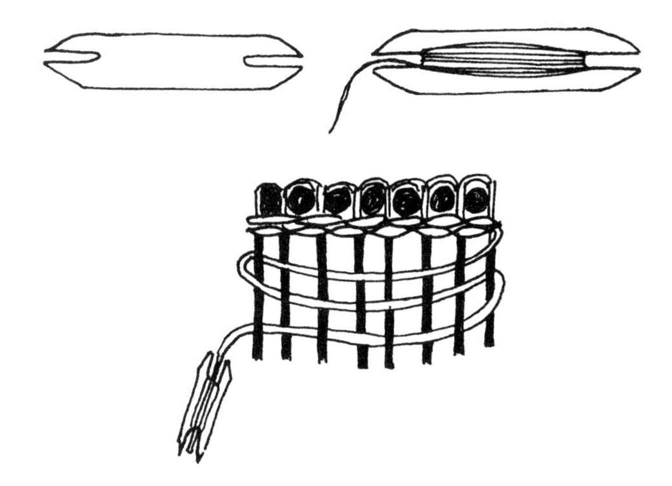

Weave backwards and forwards across the warps. Do not pull the weft too tight, but weave a few rows, then push† all the wefts up towards the top, so the weaving is firm, but not distorted. When one thread is finished, take it half way across the row, and leave to hang at the back. Start a new thread in the same place, and keep the pattern even. Trim off the ends later.

† Use a stick, or the fingers.

25 (right) Weaving a picture. Note incorporation of cotton wool and fabric strips. Boys and girls (9–10)
26 (below left) and 27 (below right) Simple tapestry weaving, dovetailing colours. Jane (10) (left). Nicholas (10) (right)

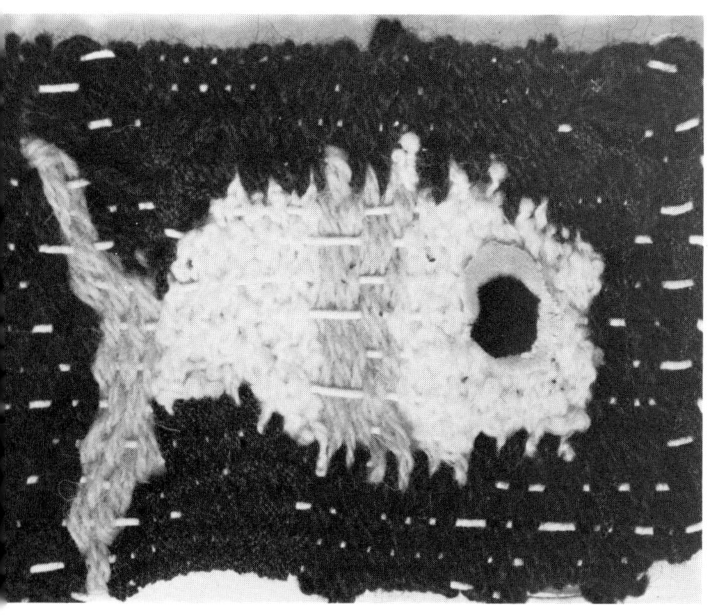

A similar loom can be made with a piece of strong card. Strengthen further by nailing a strut of wood across the back. Cut notches along the top and bottom, again 1 cm apart, or even less. Another way is to punch holes at intervals then cut through the middle of them. A tapestry weaving can be made by drawing a simple picture or pattern on the card, then when the warps are wound, the picture can be used as a guide to weaving. When the warps are wound taut, tie across the back with a secure knot.* Carry out the weaving as on the previous page, not pulling the weft too tight. Weave the shape first, then fill in the background.

* A reef knot is a secure knot.

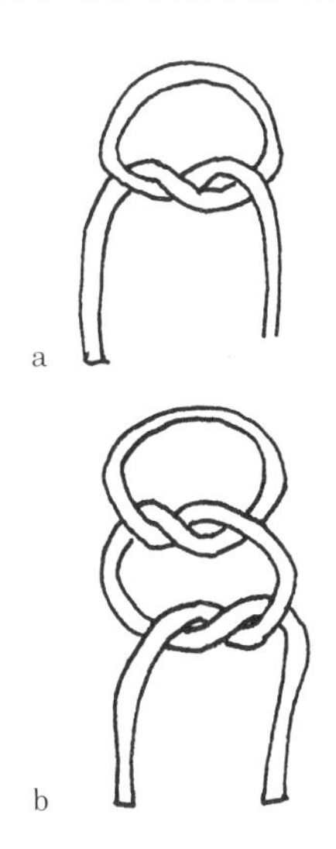

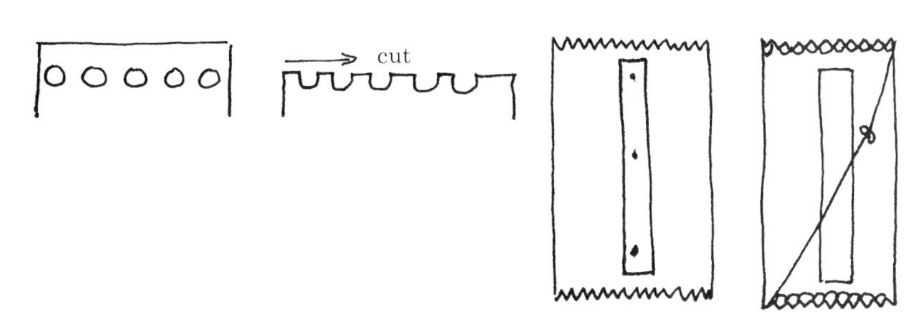

When weaving a picture, two colours come together in the middle of the work. They can be worked on their own warps independently, which leaves splits in the work where the two meet. They can also be dovetailed, so that the colours hook into each other (see illustration). Either method can be used. When the weaving is finished, lift off the nails, or loosen the knot and lift off the notches. End loops can be bent back and sewn down, or a dowel rod can be passed through the top row of end loops, and tassels** attached to the bottom loops.

** To make a tassel. Take two or three pieces of wool about 12 cm long. Bend in half, and attach one tassel to each loop. Use any thread or a mixture of threads, to match in with the hanging.

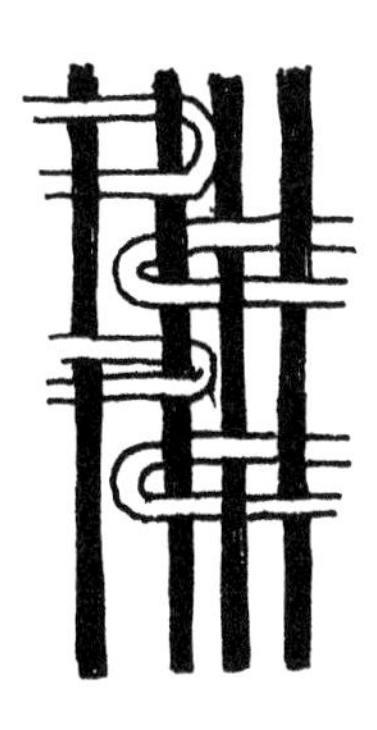

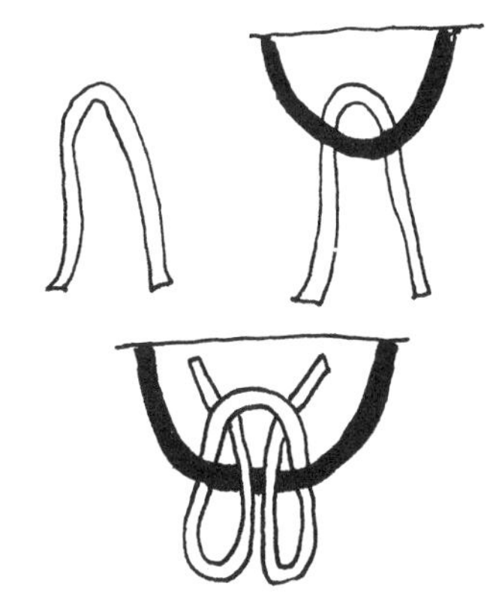

Making a round loom

On a round loom it is possible to make a bag shape (or a hat, or a puppet) in one step, without side seams. The loom is made of strong card, which should be the same size as the desired article. Notches are cut at the top and bottom as on the previous page (about 1 cm apart, or less).

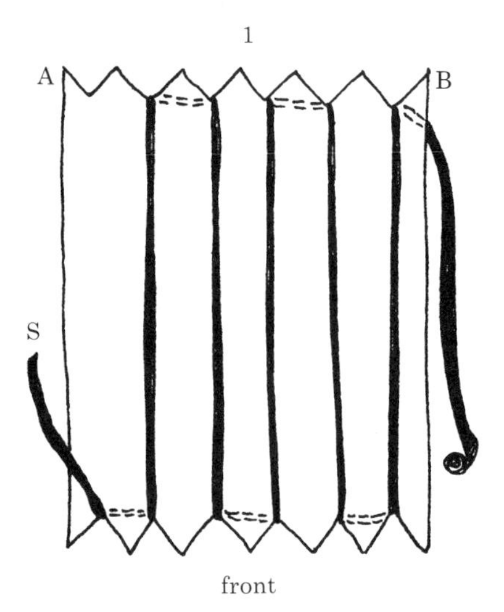

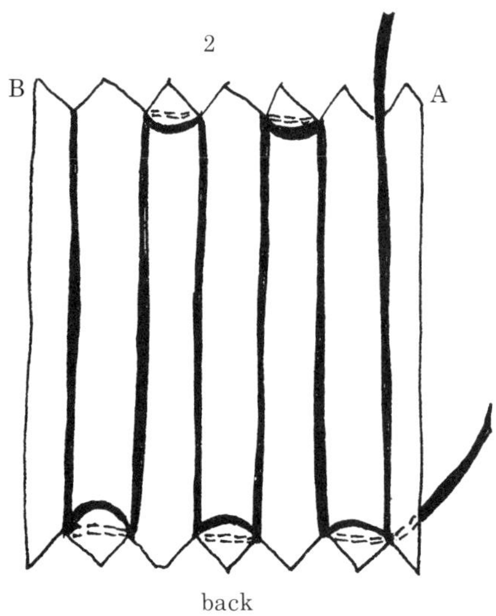

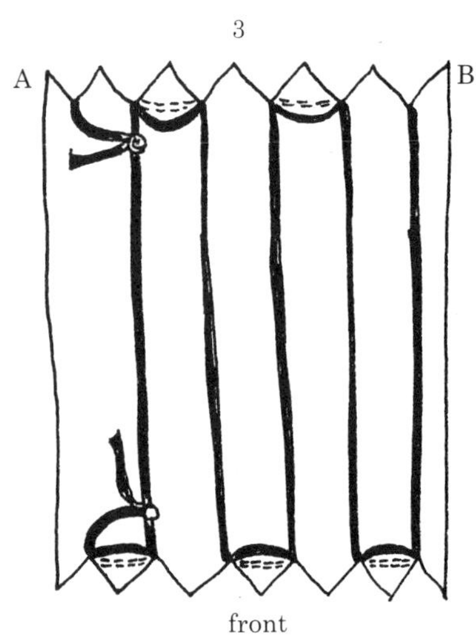

28 Erica (10)

The warps are threaded starting at S. The dotted lines indicate where the warp goes round the loom. At B, instead of finishing off, the warp is taken and threaded in a similar way, round the back of the loom, so that both sides are threaded. The warps are finished off with two half hitches, as in 3 as there must be an odd number of warps round the loom to make the weaving work out properly. This is important.

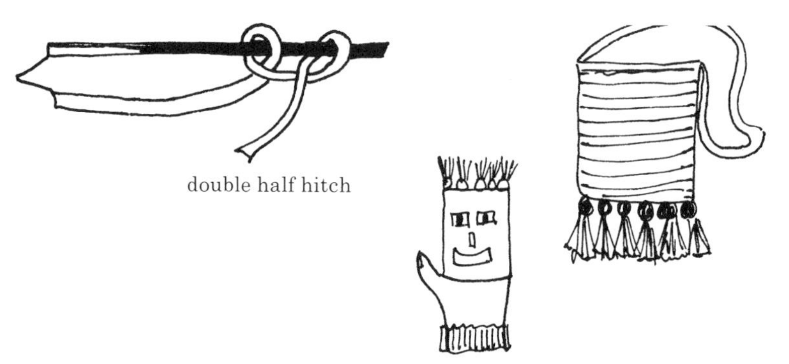

Now weave round and round the loom, forming a bag shape. Close the bottom with tassels or sew up.

Another method of making a round loom is to thread the warps horizontally, or sideways, starting at the top A, and wrapping the warp round and round the loom* (see 1).

The ends can be hooked round the next indentation, woven among the warps, and attached to a warp with a half hitch.

* The loom can be made of card, with notches at the sides to hold the warps in place. Two polystyrene tiles will make a loom, using both to give double thickness. Protect the sides with two strips of material, so that the polystyrene does not split.

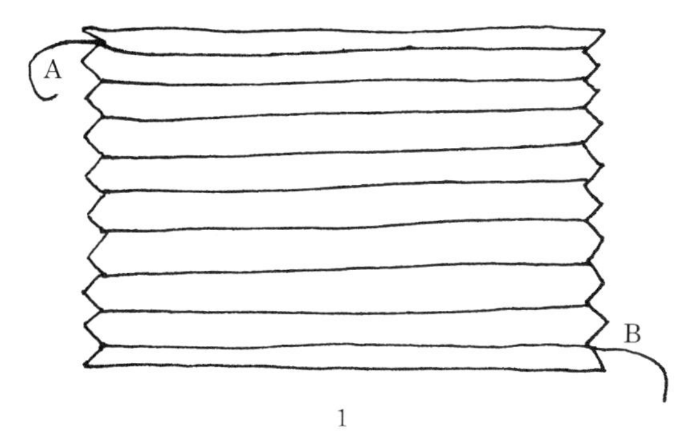

1

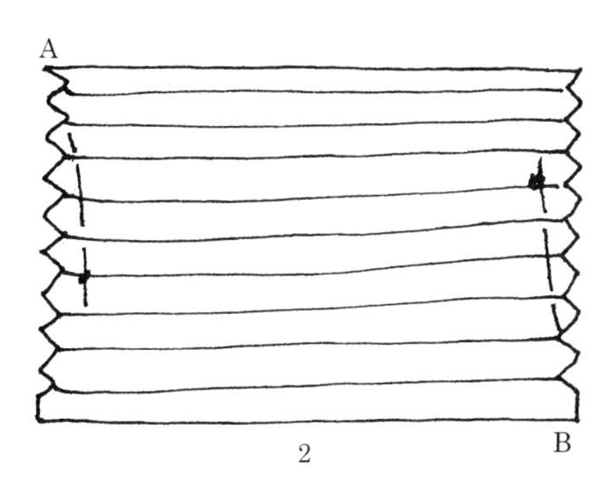

2

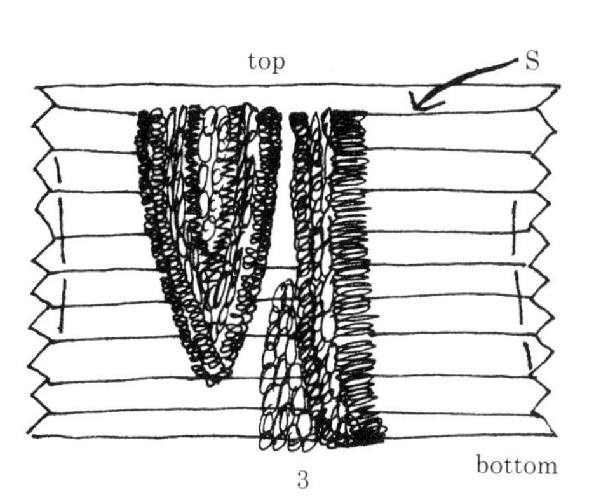

3

When the weaving is finished, the knot and the warp can be lost in the work. The weaving is done starting at S (see 3), going to the bottom of the loom, and up the opposite side to the top. This closes the bottom space, and leaves the top open. The weaving proceeds right round from the top, round the bottom to the top, then back again. The weaving can be done in different patches of colour, as long as all the space is eventually filled with weaving. Ends can be left hanging as the weaving, when taken off the loom is turned inside out.

Remember never to go over the top of the loom. When the weaving is finished, remove the loom and turn the weaving inside out. Line with fabric for a bag.

Decorating weaving

This is probably one of the most ancient methods of weaving. The warps are attached to a bar at the top, while at the bottom, they are weighted to keep them taut for weaving. The top bar* is an integral part of the hanging and should be chosen carefully. This sort of hanging looks particularly attractive if the warps, weaving threads and stone coverings, if any, are all dyed a similar colour before beginning.

* This could be the branch of a tree which has blown down, a piece of driftwood, a bamboo pole or a curtain pole.

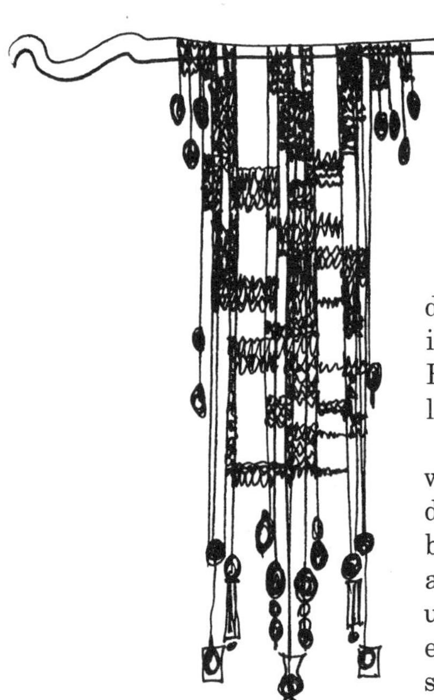

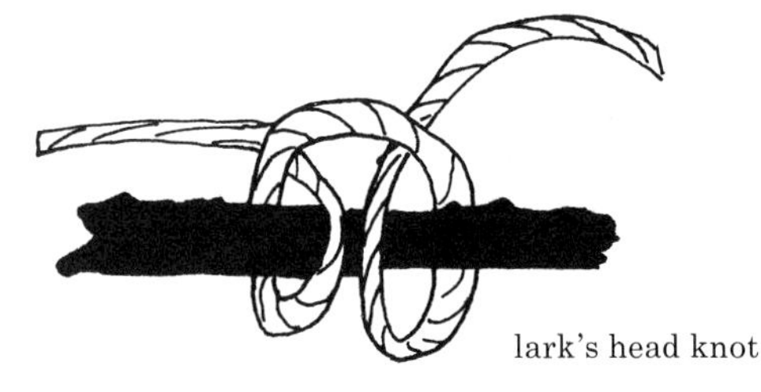

lark's head knot

Jute is a suitable warp, and dyes well. Cut each warp double the depth of the hanging. The warps can be different in length to add interest and to show off the beads or stones. Fold each warp in half and attach to the bar at the top with a lark's head knot.

The ends of the warps must now be weighted. Heavy washers† or heavy beads can be used with lighter beads for decoration. Tie a knot at the bottom of the warp to hold the beads in position. If it seems that there are too many beads and washers jostling together, shorten some of the warps or use a single weight for two warps. Stones are cheaper and easier to come by than heavy beads. Smooth stones can be suspended in a sort of bag which can be made from a suitable piece of fabric. Cut a piece of fabric bigger than the pebble (see 1). Draw it into a bag round the stone and slip over the end of the knotted warp. Tie tightly above the knot (see 3). Bind up over the spare fabric and tie at the top (see 4) or use a rubber band (see 5).

† Washers can be bound with thread to make them look pretty.

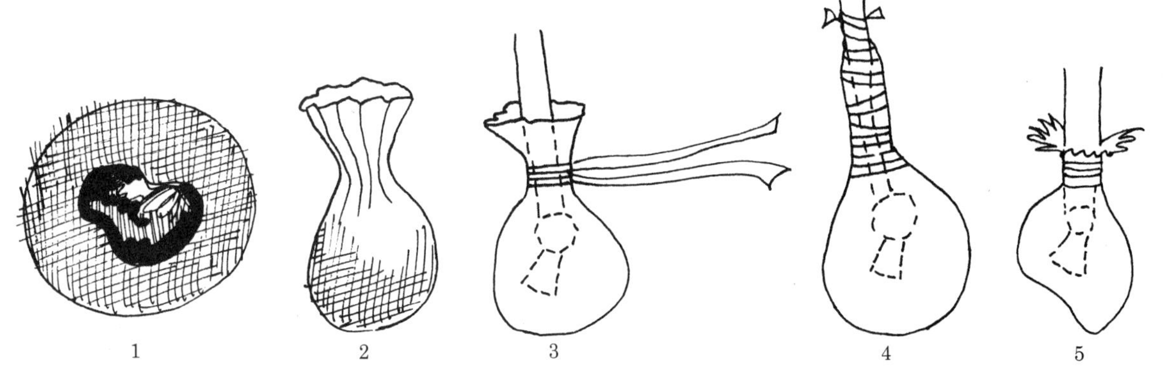

29 Boys and girls (6–10)

Rough stones can be attached with string, which can then be decorated with weaving. Flint looks particularly attractive, and has plenty of angles to hold the warp secure.

Now weave freely over the warps, pushing the wefts up with the fingers and using a cardboard shuttle (see page 39). There is no need to weave over all the warps and some can be left showing. (That is why it is a good idea to dye the warps to match the threads so that they will all fit in together.) Leave some holes and add tassels and beads.

While weaving, the hanging can be suspended by tying a piece of string to each end of the bar and hanging from a hook, or suitably positioned nail.

These hangings can be used as a decoration over a doorway, or they can be made on quite a small scale, on a twig, or a small bar. They can also be constructed on the bough of a tree and left as a permanent fixture. If there is no tree around, use one end of a climbing frame. However, outdoor hangings should be made from durable materials like string and rope.

Weaving on a double warp is more difficult, but very effective. In this method the loom itself is an integral part of the hanging. It can be made from a picture frame,* or from four pieces of wood joined at the corners with a mitre joint, so that the frame is rigid.

The warp is wound round and round the loom. Secure the ends with two half hitches (see 1). The warp must be tight, so use strong thread. If the warps slip, hold with drawing pins in the back of the frame, so they do not show. Remove at the end. Now the loom has threads at both sides, so weaving can be done on the front, then the loom turned and more weaving can be done on the back. When the work is finished, the weaving will look three dimensional. Try to make the weaving as interesting as possible, using different textures and colours. Remember that it should be possible to look through the weaving on the front to the weaving at the back, so the two should look well together. The weaving on the front warps can be kept open and lacy.

* A stretcher for oil painting, or a strong picture frame.
The loom can be stained a suitable colour, or strips or material or thread can be wound round and round to cover the wood, or you can leave the wood in a natural state, and choose suitable colours or string, and use wooden beads or pine cones for decoration.

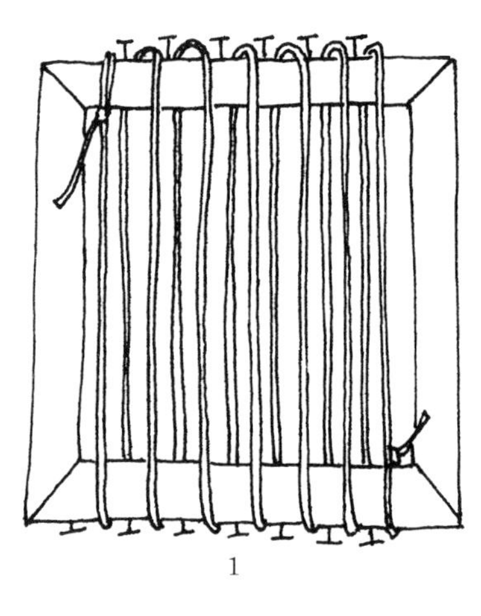

1

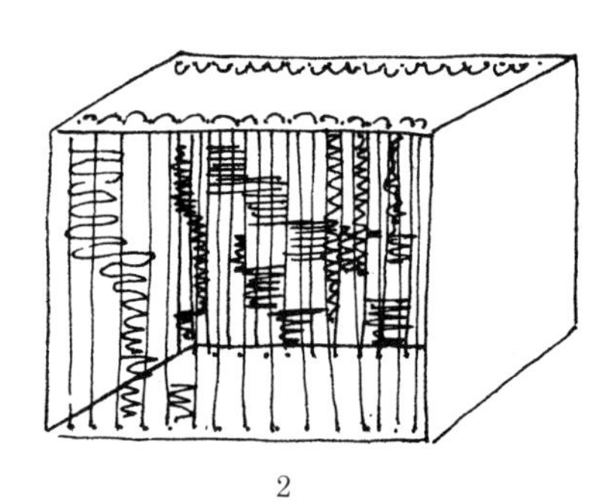

2

A much more complicated loom can be made with four pieces of wood or perspex** (see 2). Holes are drilled along the edge, front and back at the top and bottom. Join the edges and make an open box. The weaving is done on warps threaded in the holes at front and back. This is rather like a peep show.

** Nylon fishing line fits in well with perspex.

A loom can be made from four pieces of branch.* Join the corners of the branch with square lashing (see below). Make sure this is really tight.

Now wind the warp round as before. Make sure it is taut.

It will be difficult to keep the tension even, so warps can be attached in two pieces, from middle to sides, or the warps can be attached individually.

* Driftwood or tree prunings. Choose fairly straight pieces. The bark can either be stripped or left on.

** The string should be strong. Try jute twine.

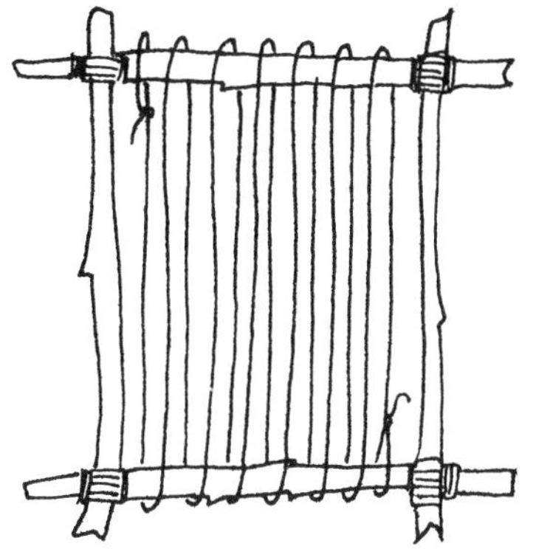

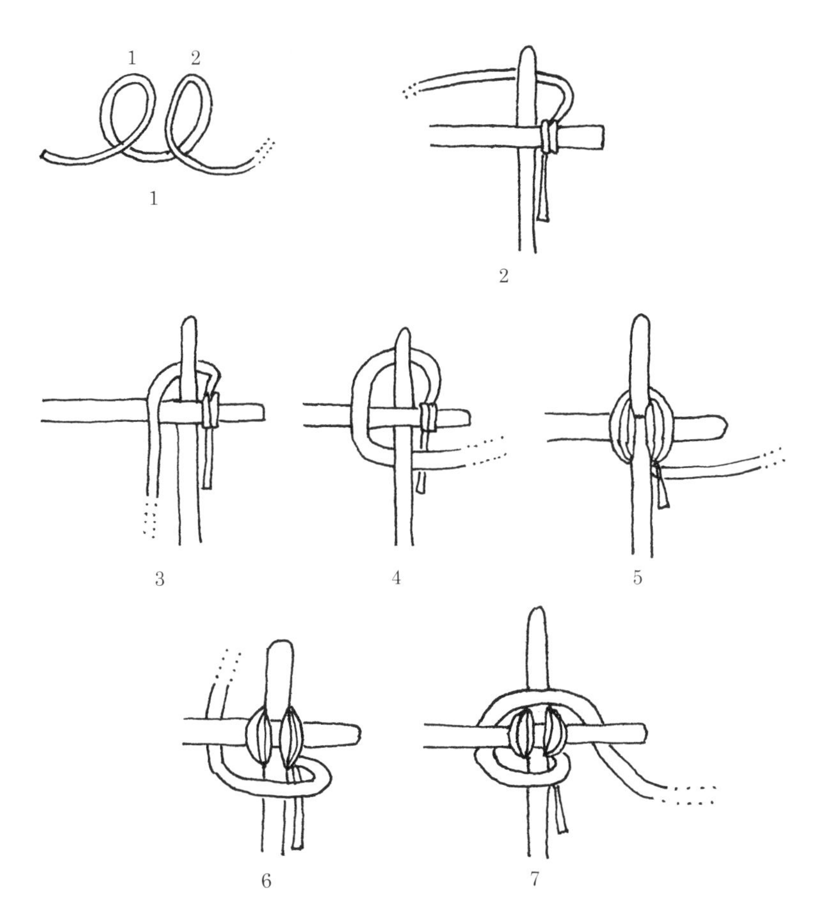

To square lash two branches

A piece of string** at least 60–70 cm long. Make two loops opposite ways, next to each other (see 1) and put loop 1 over loop 2.

With one branch behind and at right angles to the other, put loops over end and pull tight, short end by branch (see 2). Wind long end round branch, under, over, under, over (see 2, 3, 4), continue (1, 2, 3, 4), three times ending at position in diagram 5. Go back, but now over, under, over, under, (see 6 and 7) three times.

Tie ends together with a reef knot. Repeat at each corner.

30 Caroline (12)

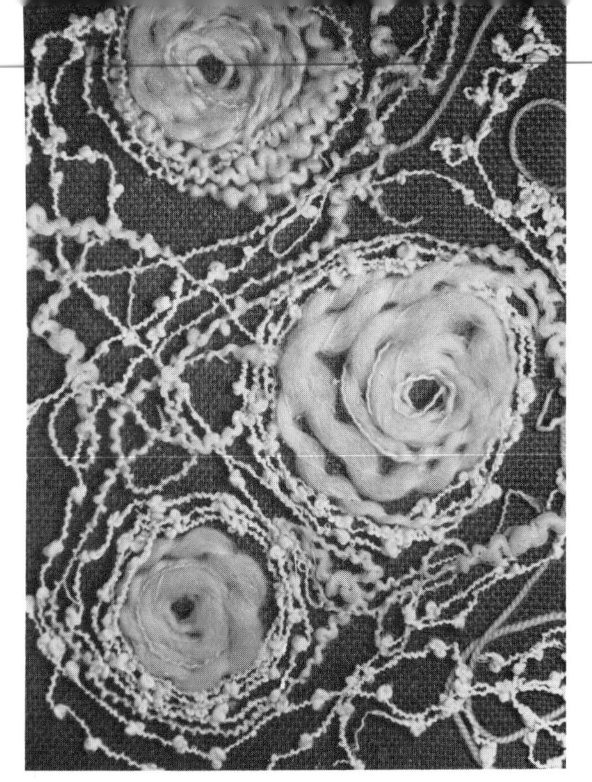

31 Collage with weaving yarns. Richard (10)

32 String collage. Cecile (13)

Using string

Collect as many different varieties of string* as possible, to look at and discuss. String is used in a large variety of ways, and it might be interesting to talk about what each piece of string in the collection is made from, and how it can be used.

* If possible, include pieces of white string, which is made of cotton; brown string, made of jute. The more hairy, cheaper brown string is more likely to be made of hemp. Sisal string is often dyed green for use in horticulture. Cotton, jute, hemp can be bought polished or unpolished. Polished string has a shiny smooth finish. Unpolished looks dull, and feels softer. When dyeing string choose unpolished, as it will take the colour of the dye much more readily. It is also possible to get plastic string. It is interesting to see all the different sorts of string and rope at a rope and string manufacturer.

Handle the string, and smell it. Some is rough and some is smooth. String is made up of bundles** of much thinner fibres which have been twisted together. Take three or four different types and thicknesses of string and fray out the ends. Count the bundles, then see how many fibres make a bundle. Now try to break the fibres. Which string has the stronger fibres? Although the fibres themselves will break, when they are twisted in bundles they are very strong. Try to break a piece of string.

** A bundle is called a ply (one ply, two ply, three ply, etc).

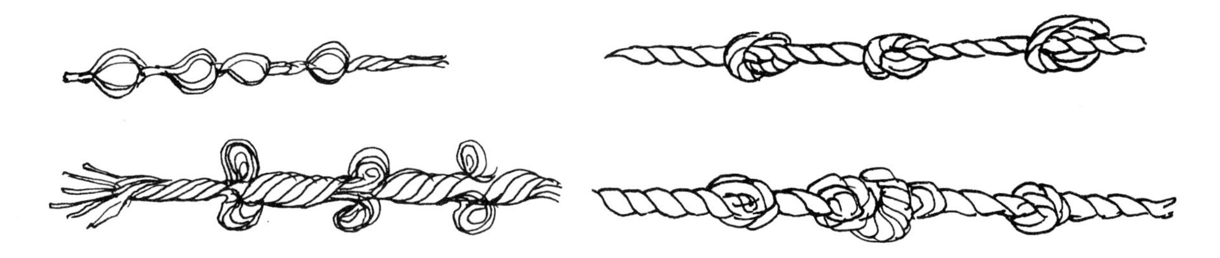

Now take several thicknesses of string, and make slubs in it by pulling it apart with the finger nails along the length of the string. Compare the slubs made in different sorts of string. Make some small, and some quite big. Make slubs by tying knots at intervals along the string. Tie some knots far apart and some close together. Put two pieces of string together, and tie knots along both. Make a hanging on a stick with the pieces of knotted string. Hang a bead at the bottom of each as a weight, and fray out the end into a tassel.

Unravel some of the string completely. Using various thicknesses of string, and some of the unravelled string, make patterns.* Use one, two or several thicknesses of unravelled string to make lines. Try crossing pieces of string. Use thick and thin pieces. Cut pieces and make patterns with small pieces.

* Use a strong glue to stick string.

Background can and should be varied. Try tweed, hessian, furnishing fabric.

Paste onto cardboard or hardboard.

Try dyeing string in hot water dye.

Make the string flow in curves. Twist it back over itself. Make circles, big and small, thin and fat, some touching and some apart. Take a simple shape. Make the string go round and round it. Make the string curl and curve. Make small straight patterns, knobbly and curved patterns. Make slubs and knots. Now try to make a string picture of a bird or an animal or a person. Try to use all the different patterns which the string will make. Use pasta and wooden beads as these look attractive with string.

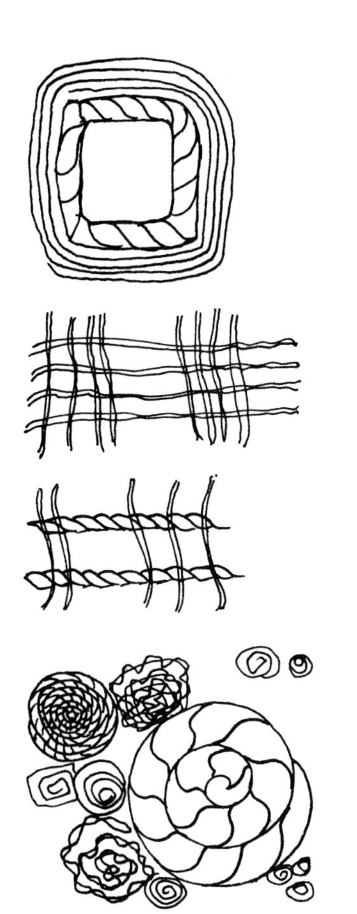

FABRIC AND THREAD USED TOGETHER

Needles

There is a large selection of needles on the market. Traditionally, *crewel* needles are made for embroidery, and *sharps* for dressmaking. However, this is because the eye of a crewel needle is long, and will take several strands of embroidery cotton, while a *sharp* or *between* has a small eye suitable for sewing cotton. Nowadays, we use all sorts of different threads in embroidery, sometimes including string and strips of material, so a needle should be chosen because the thread will pass easily through the eye, and does not keep falling out. Generally, blunt needles are used in work where the needle passes between the weft and warp of the background fabric,* and sharp needles are used for work where the background is pierced with the needle.

* As when using canvas, and also in weaving and needleweaving.

Suede and leather are difficult to pierce with an ordinary needle, so use a *leather*, or *glover's* needle. This has a triangular sharpened point which passes more easily through the background. Very thin needles with thin eyes are specially made for sewing on tiny beads. These are *beading* needles.

It is now possible to buy *ball point* needles for use on jersey fabrics made of nylon and acrylic fibres. These needles have blunted ends which do not catch in the fabric.

A *carpet* needle** might be useful for very thick wool or string. Semi-circular needles are used when it is impossible to catch a piece of fabric with a straight needle.

** Also useful for applying glue.

Store needles in a damp-proof box. Try to keep them pinned in order of size on a piece of flannel, or put them back into their wrappings. The black paper protects them from damp and rust.

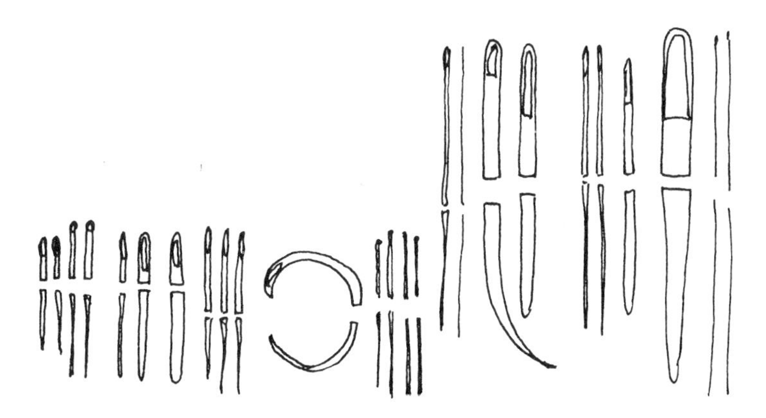

Frames

In work with fabric and thread, it is sometimes necessary to use a frame to keep the fabric taut. There are several different types, including the traditional slate frame, which is excellent for an experienced embroiderer, but not very suitable for use in school.

The round frame, or hoop, in various sizes can be most useful. It is in two parts. The outer circle has a screw to loosen and tighten. The inner circle should be bound with bias binding. This helps to hold the cloth in place, and prevents the wood from catching and marking the fabric.

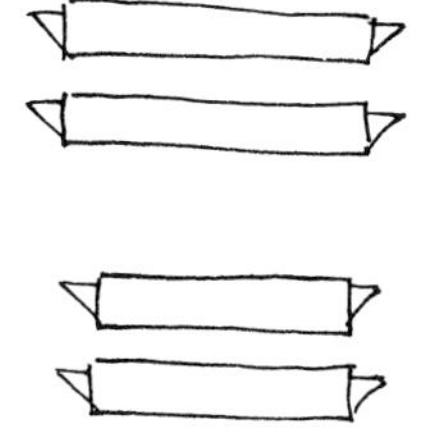

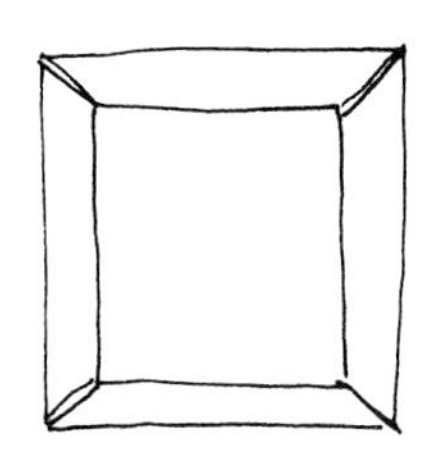

The square frame is one of the most versatile frames, and not made in the first place for work with fabric and thread. It is made from the stretchers used to stretch canvas ready for oil painting. These stretchers are sold in various sizes or lengths, and the frame is assembled by slotting together the mitred corners. Small wedges hold the frame rigid, if necessary. The frame should be assembled so that the work area fits into the inner dimensions of the square. It is sometimes possible to pin* the work straight onto the frame, but drawing pins sometimes rust or mark the background. If this is likely to happen, and if it matters, pin a piece of sheeting** or calico onto the frame (pin at the back). Now sew the piece of work onto the calico with running stitches. When work is done, stitches go through both background and sheeting. Cut extra calico or sheeting away. The material stretched on the frame should be taut, but not so taut that it distorts. Have the material straight with weft and warp running parallel with the frame. Try to tack work on with weft and warp going the same way as the backing.

* Drawing pins or staples.

** Any thin, strong fabric, which does not have to be new.

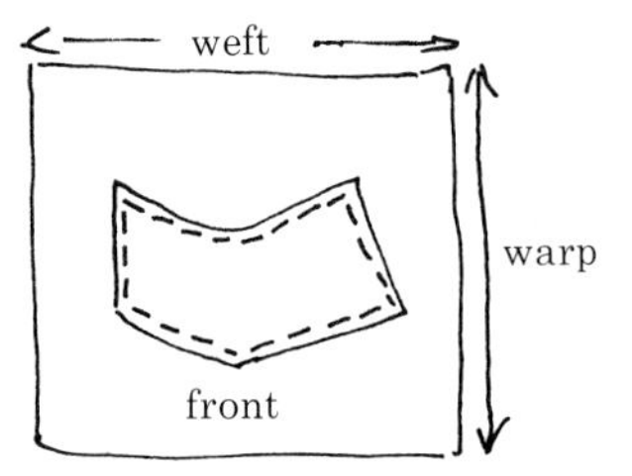

Running stitch

Choose some threads which are a different weight from each other, but the same colour (use different tones).

Cotton, wool, stranded cotton, thick wool, rug wool, raffia, string.

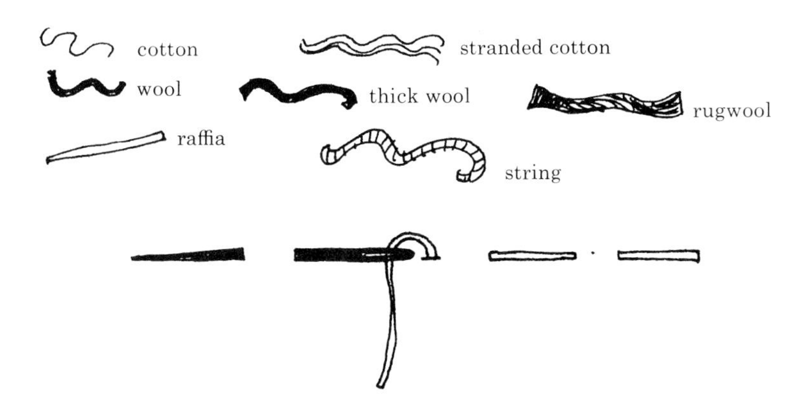

Find a background* which looks interesting with the chosen threads for whatever reason. Now try to stitch on the fabric with running stitch.

* Backgrounds for stitching can be virtually any fabric. It is best to choose something which is easy to manage at first, and which does not stretch. However it is important to experiment on all types of material to see what they look like.

Method

Start with a knot, but do not wet the fingers. This dirties the thread. Leave some thread which can be woven in afterwards if necessary.

Try large and small stitches in different threads.

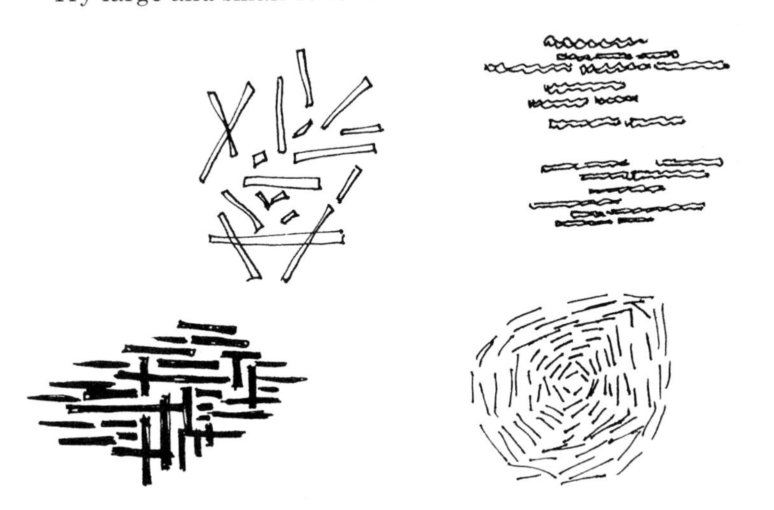

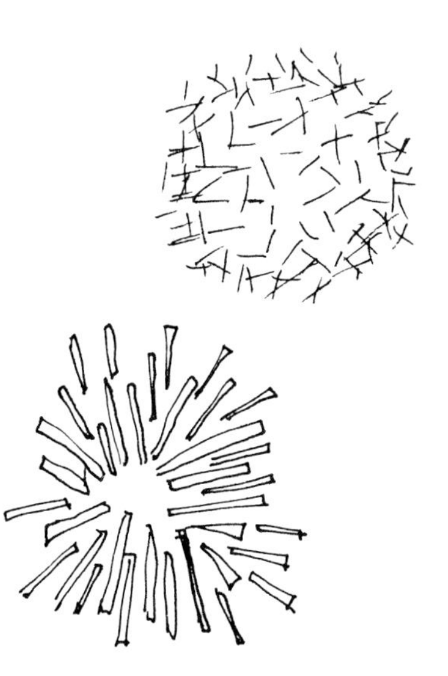

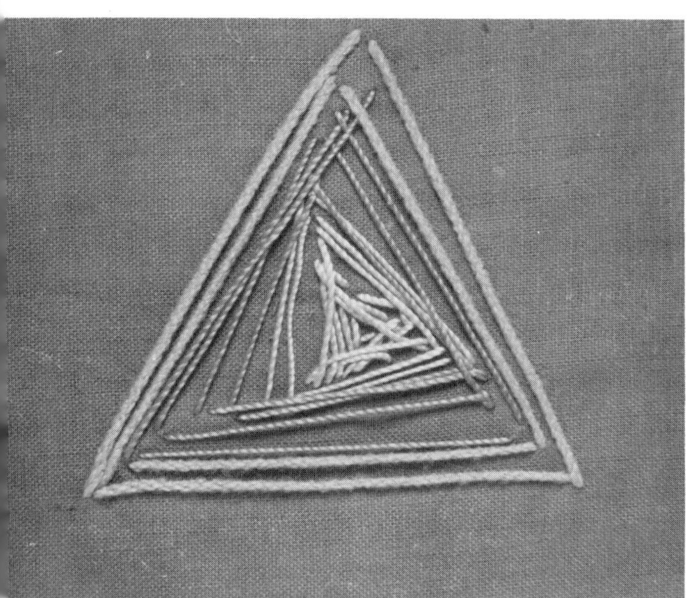

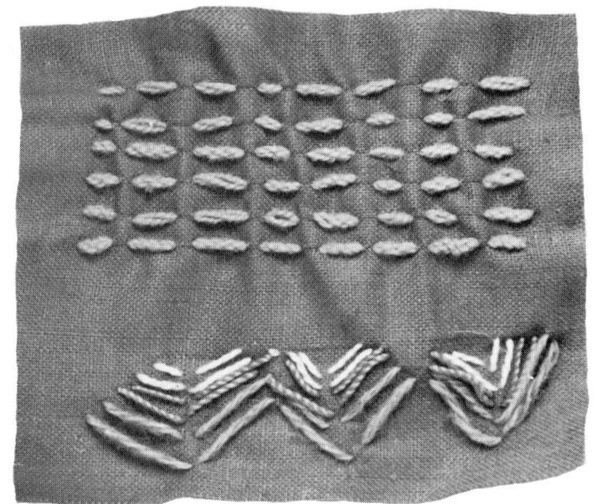

33–37 First experiments with running stitch making patterns. Boys and girls (8)

Make large and small stitches. Make spiky, rounded and curved patterns. Use different threads. Try different threads together.

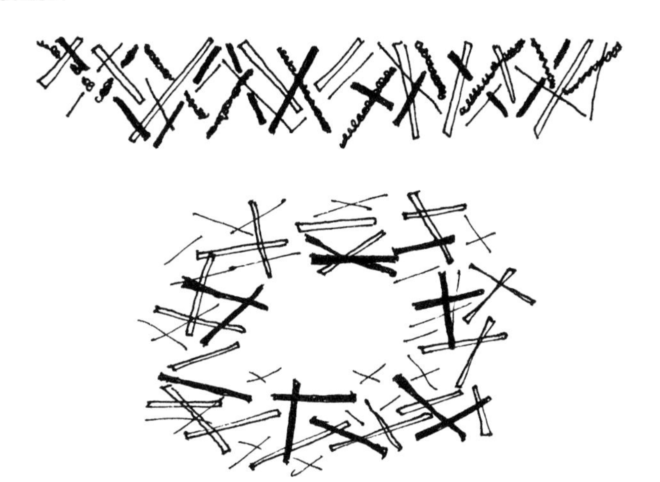

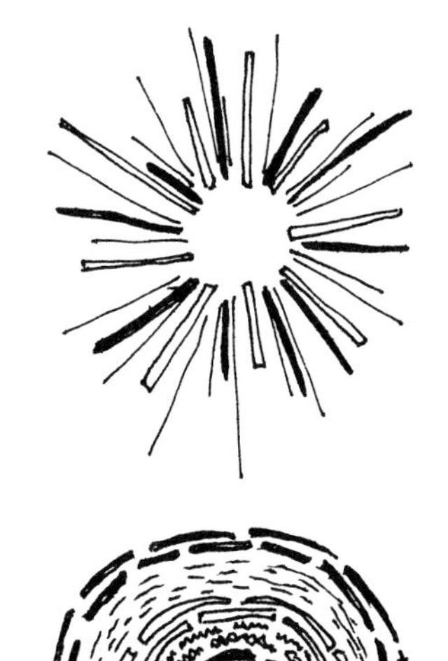

Use light and dark backgrounds. Use patterned and textured backgrounds. Try to keep the background flat by not pulling the threads too tight. Try to experiment with different patterns and threads.

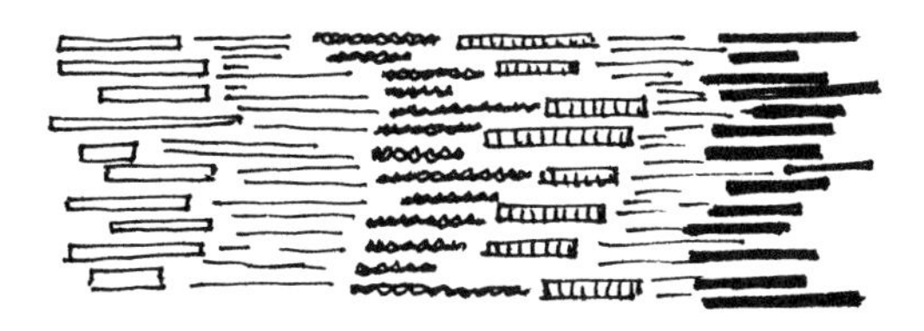

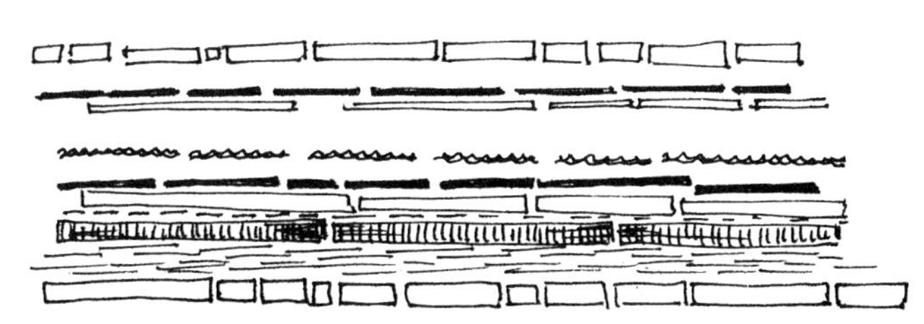

To finish off, weave thread into the back of the fabric. Do not pull. These sorts of experiment can be used with any embroidery stitch. The important thing is to learn thoroughly how one stitch behaves with various fabrics and threads, before passing onto the next.

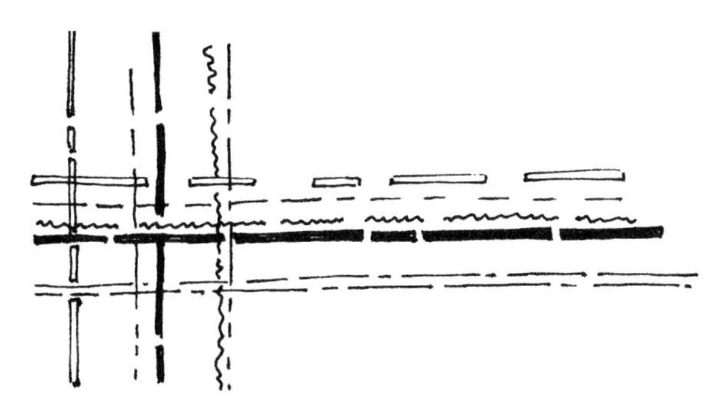

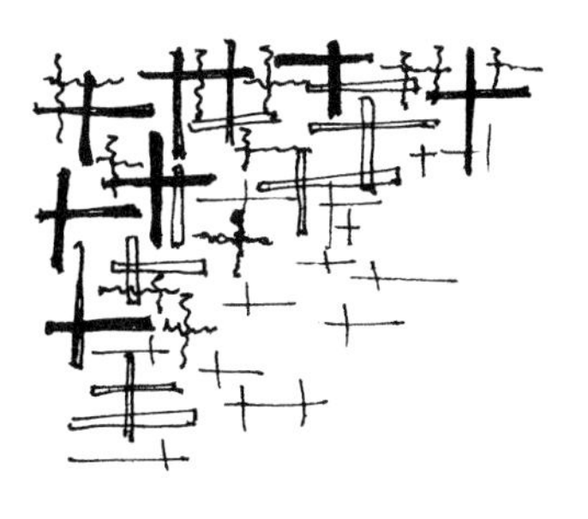

Appliqué

The last page was all about making patterns with stitches. Sometimes a fabric shape might be needed, and instead of sticking the shape down with glue, it might be more decorative to attach it with stitches. This is called *appliqué*.

The simplest way of doing appliqué is to cut out the shape with very sharp scissors, tack* it onto the background,** and sew round the edge with running stitches. Do not turn in the edges at this stage.

* Tacking stitch is a big straight stitch, or running stitch, used to hold fabric in place.

** Use a fairly strong fabric which will not stretch. Hessian, denim, crash, etc. If the background is not firm enough, stiffen with dressmakers' interfacing.

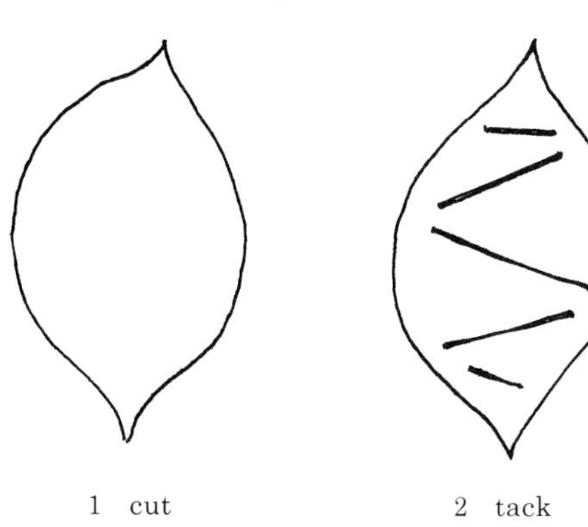

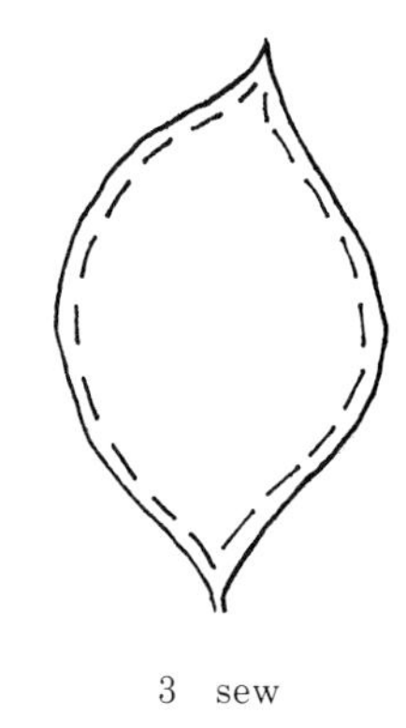

1 cut   2 tack   3 sew

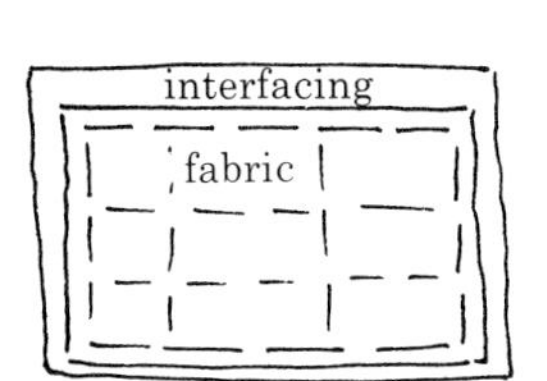

Use ordinary sewing cotton for running stitch. Tie a knot at the end of the thread before sewing.

It is interesting to experiment with different patterned and plain fabric in appliqué. Make use of patterns on fabric; try patterned† backgrounds, striped backgrounds and check backgrounds instead of plain fabric. Try light on dark and dark on light.

† Patterned cottons, and cotton/polyester might be used, so stiffen with interfacing.
Tack round the edge and across to hold.

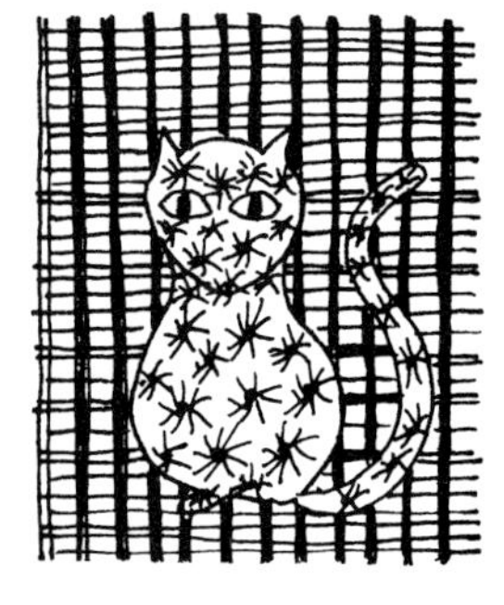

Now the applied shapes can be decorated with stitches. To practise, start with a very simple shape, and cut out several. Try out different ways of decorating the shapes with straight* stitches. The stitches do not have to be even. Any thread can be used, as long as it will go through the background and the applied shape. Try different threads** to see which look best. Make the stitches go in different directions. Make them cross each other. Do some tiny stitches and some big. Make some come over the edge onto the background.

* Or other stitches, as they are mastered.

** Try sewing cotton, stranded cotton, crochet cotton, wools, metallic thread, embroidery threads.

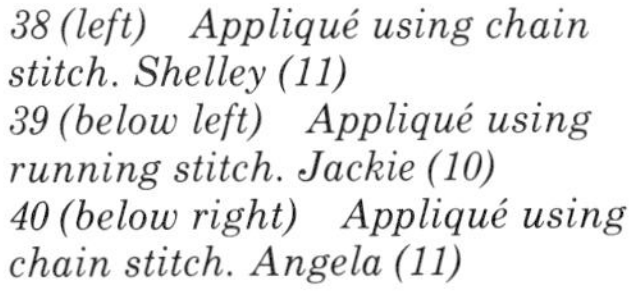

38 (left) Appliqué using chain stitch. Shelley (11)
39 (below left) Appliqué using running stitch. Jackie (10)
40 (below right) Appliqué using chain stitch. Angela (11)

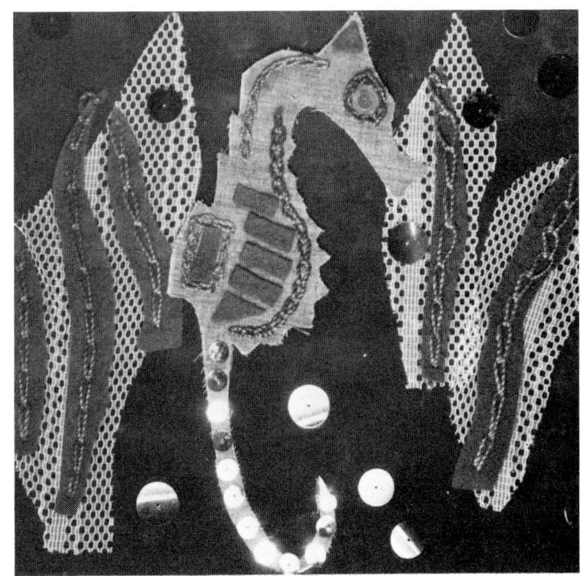

It is possible to make an applied picture more interesting if some of the shapes or figures can be padded to raise them from the background. This is quite simply done by putting a little kapok* underneath the shape before it is sewn to the background, or while it is being sewn to the background.

* Terylene wadding may also be used. It can be cut into shapes more easily than kapok. Cotton wool is not suitable as it goes lumpy.

Method one

1 Kapok is pulled into a shape a little smaller than the fabric shape.

2 The kapok is laid on the background and the fabric shape is tacked on top of it.

3 The shape is stitched onto the background and the tacking stitches are taken out.

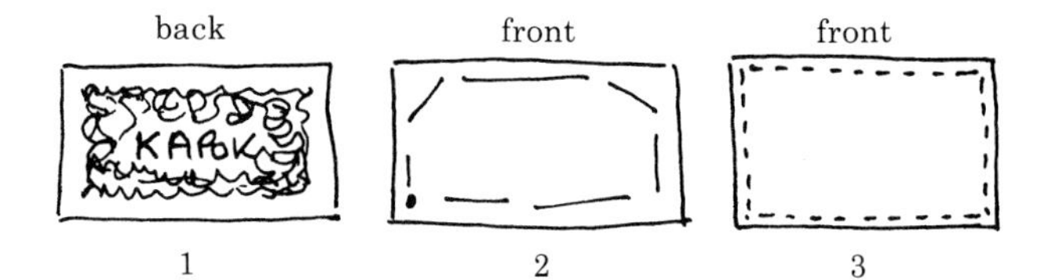

Method two

1 The fabric shape is tacked onto the background.

2 The shape is stitched on three sides. The kapok is then pushed under the shape with a knitting needle.

3 The stitches are then continued along the fourth side of the shape. When the shape has been padded, it can be decorated with small straight** stitches, which will make dimples in the padded fabric. Use sewing cotton for this. Tie a knot in the end. This is also called *quilting*.

** Running stitch.

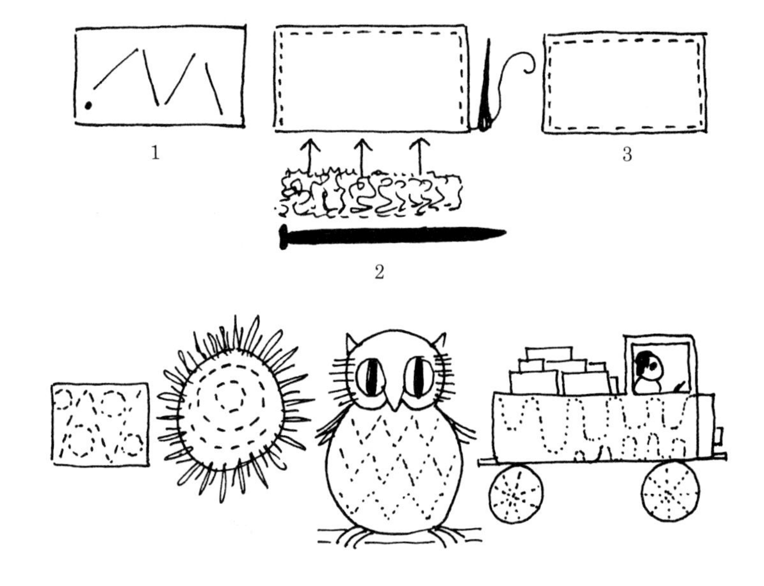

41 Donna (9)

Padded shapes

Small padded shapes can be made separately, and sewn or stuck onto the picture afterwards.

1 Circles. Cut circles* of material** (not too small). Make a knot at the end of the thread. Make running stitches round the edge (not too near or it will fray). Leave the end of thread. Take out the needle.

* Freehand.

** Use something like cotton, which is soft, easy to manage and does not slip.

1

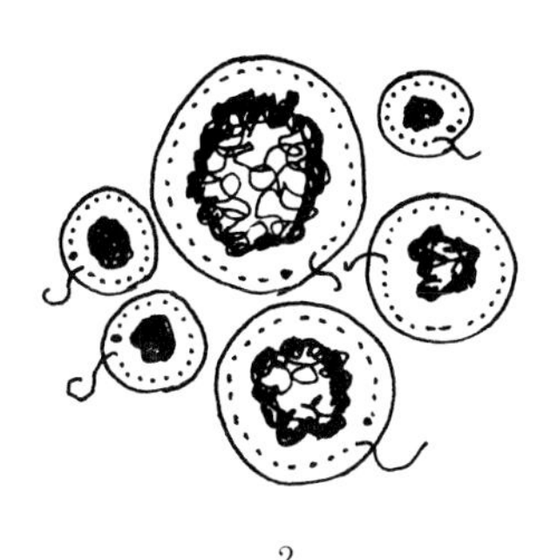

2

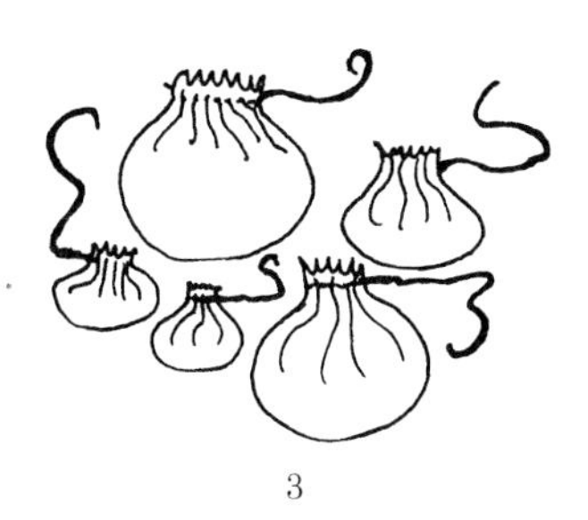

3

2 Put a small pad of kapok† in the middle of the circle.

3 Pull the end of the thread and make a bag. Pull it tight to close the neck. Turn the bag upside down. Using the end of the thread, thread the needle, and pull the thread through the background to attach the bag. Take the needle back and through the neck of the bag to tighten and strengthen. The bag could also be stuck on the background instead of sewing.

Other shapes (triangles, rectangles, scales). It is a good idea to make these shapes in felt or other material which will not fray.

† Or a round piece of card or felt, terylene wadding or shredded nylon tights.

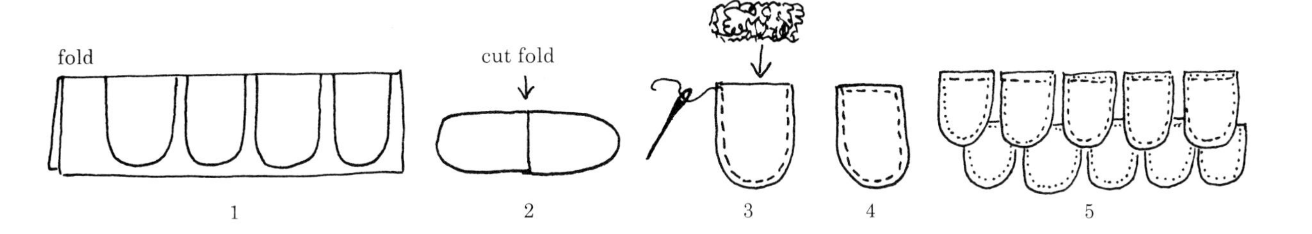

1 Fold material. Cut out shape on fold.

2 Cut across fold.

3 Running stitch round three sides of shape, stuff with kapok and

4 Running stitch across the end.

These shapes can be sewn or stuck in overlapping rows. They can also be made in different shapes and sizes.

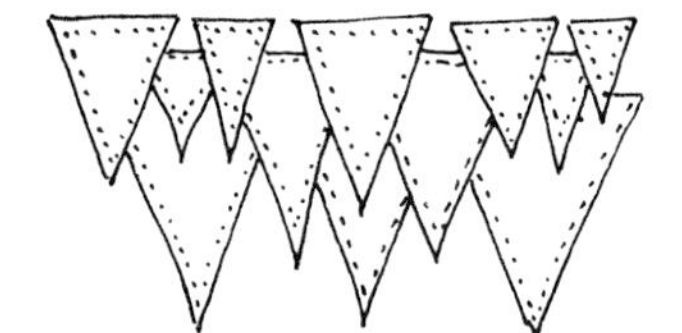

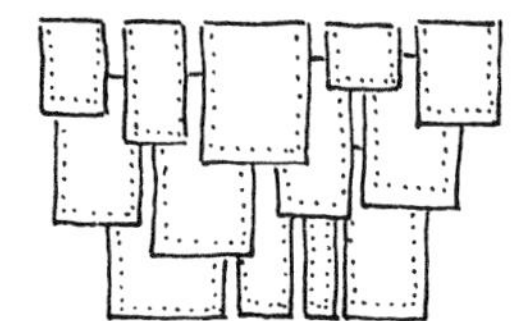

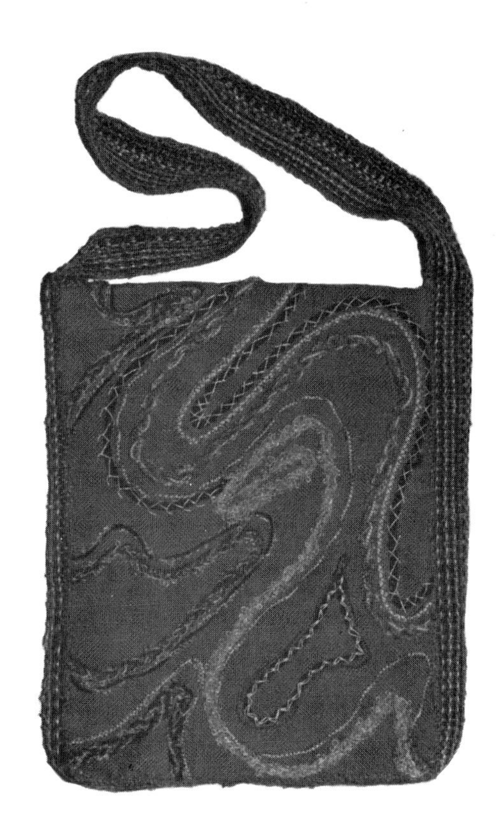

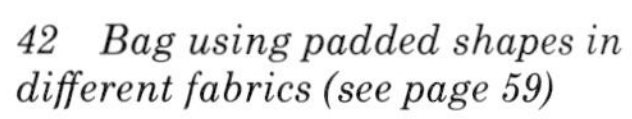

42 Bag using padded shapes in different fabrics (see page 59)

43 Bag using couched threads (see pages 61–62) Girls (12–15)

Slub yarns

There are many interesting and beautiful yarns which will not go through a needle, and because they are covered with slubs and knots they cannot be pulled through a background. This is also true of metallic yarns and thick wools, if the chosen background happens to have a fine weave.

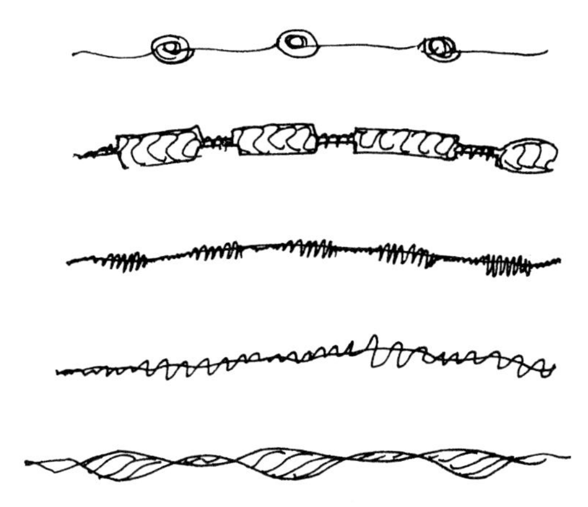

Couching

Therefore these fancy yarns and thick threads have to be attached to the background by a method called couching.

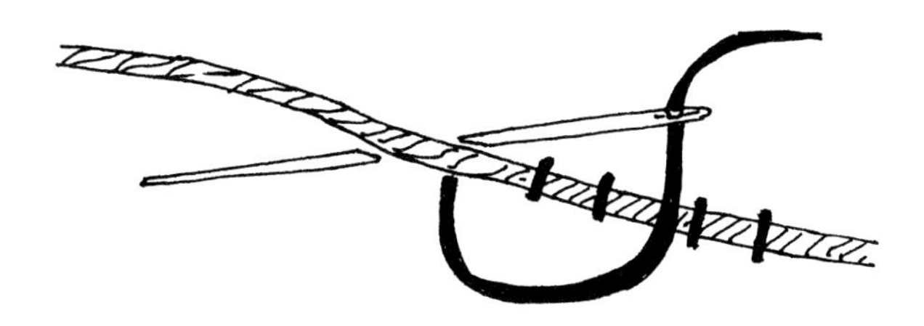

1 Start with a knot* at the back of the fabric.
2 Hold the thread to be couched with one hand and sew a little stitch across at intervals, to hold the thread down.

Although the couched threads can be pinned or tacked to the background before couching it is much easier to indicate the line the couched thread will follow with some sort of marking.**

However, to begin, and for practise, just couch at random, using as many different yarns as possible to see how they look. Because this work can be quite weighty when a lot of thick threads are couched onto the background, it is much easier to do it on a frame (see page 52).

Balance the frame between a chair-back and the edge of a table, then sit at the frame. Both hands are then free.

* Use a thread which will match the couched threads.

** Do not use lead pencil as it smudges. Use dressmakers' chalk, or dressmakers' pencil. Poster, powder and watercolour paint can also be used to paint a line as thin as possible, with a fine brush. Use a colour which can only just be seen.

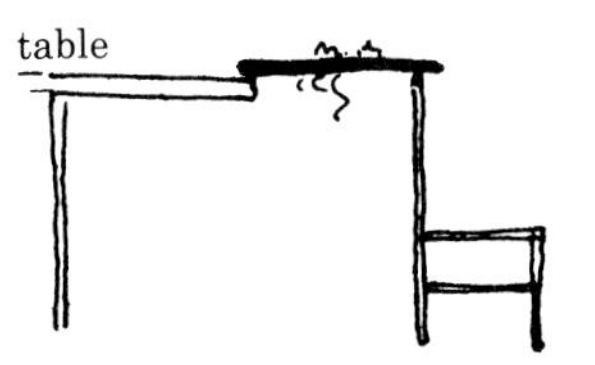

Although couching stitches are often as unobtrusive as possible, so that the fancy yarns are not spoiled, it is sometimes interesting to make the couching threads themselves part of the pattern.

Experiment by stitching with colours different from the couched yarn.

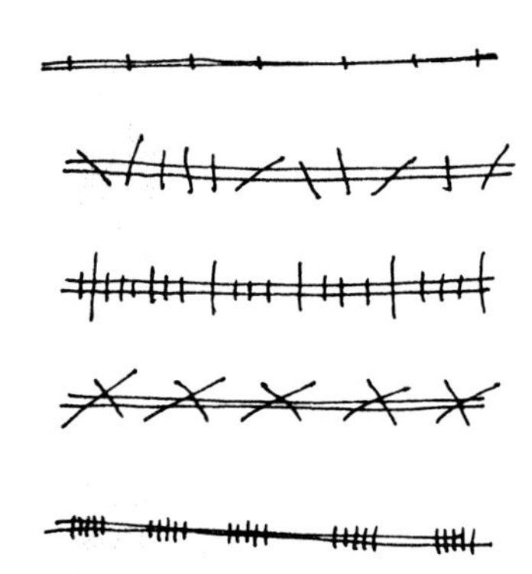

Try making the stitches into different patterns. Put the stitches at different angles, and make the stitches different sizes. Couching makes it possible to sew any sort of thread onto a background.* Use 'made' threads, like strips of leather, corduroy, tights. Use string, rug wool, several strands of wool together. Tie knots in threads. Look out for interesting yarns, ribbons and strings.

It is possible to couch strings of beads, plaits, braids and cords.

* Any background can be used as long as it does not stretch. If it is thin, back it with dressmakers' interfacing.

Paper backed hessian is strong.

Back material with paper, using cellulose paste.

Gathering

Take a piece of fabric* and a length of sewing cotton. Tie a knot at the end of the cotton, and make a line of running stitches across the middle of the fabric. Take the needle out, then pull the end of the cotton so that the material gathers. See what the material looks like when it is gathered just a little, then when it is pulled up tight.

* Cotton, polyester/cotton, any fairly fine fabric.

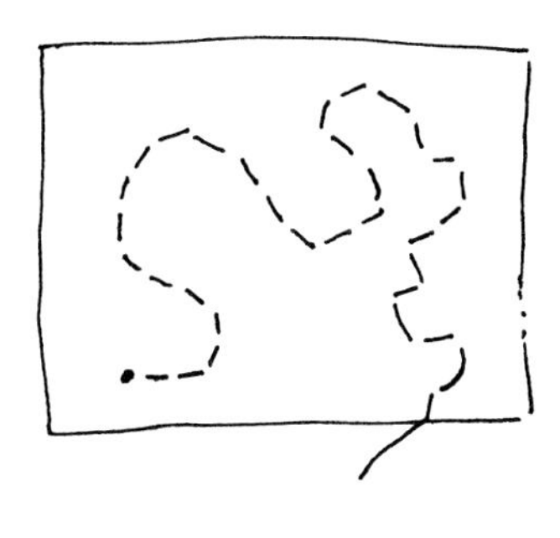

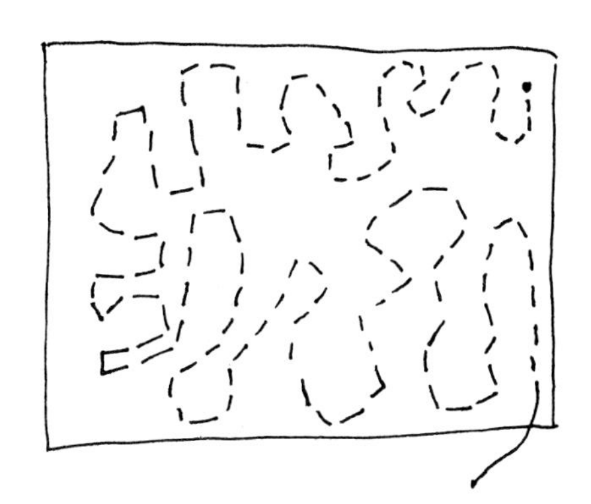

Next, try making gathers all over a piece of material to give it an interesting texture. See what happens when big stitches are used, and when small stitches are used. When gathering random patterns, it is easier to gather the material as the work progresses, otherwise the thread will be too long, and might break. Make a few stitches, then gather, both loosely and tightly. To finish, take thread to the back, and take two or three stitches into the background, to stop the thread from coming out. Always use a reasonably strong thread, and choose a colour to merge in with the background. See the effects of gathering on velvet, satin, taffeta, rayon, etc.

So that the stitches show on the front as little as possible, work on the back of the fabric, and only pick up a little piece of fabric for each stitch.

Gathering in lines
Experiment with different length, but even, stitches and also make gathering stitches near together, and far apart.

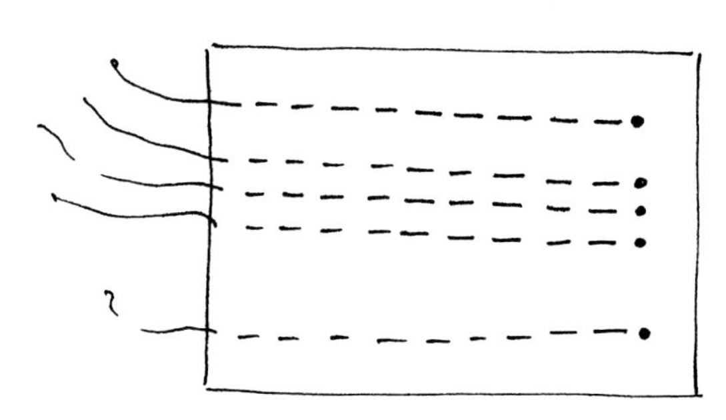

* Spots, stripes, checks, tiny patterns in regular lines.

** Squares, circles, rectangles, triangles.

Try using fabric with even patterns* to gather on, which help to make even stitches. Find some fabric with even patterns. Cut this into shapes,** using the pattern to help. Gather one line of running stitches across each. Gather gently. Fasten off at the back. Arrange the three-dimensional shapes in patterns, or use them as decorations for a picture. Find as many patterns as possible, and try out different shapes.

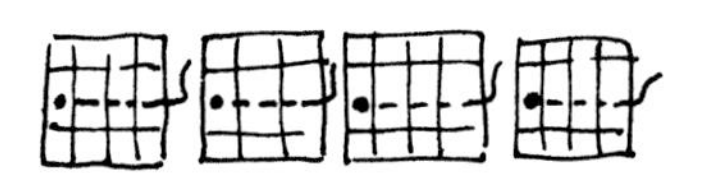

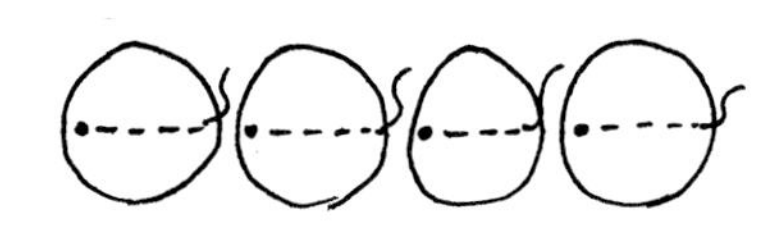

Gathering in circles. No compasses. Gather circles of running stitches. Fasten off each as it is finished. Make circles close together and far apart, big and small.

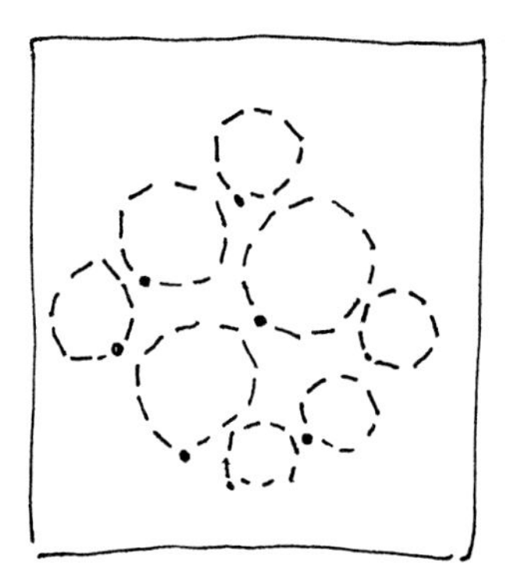

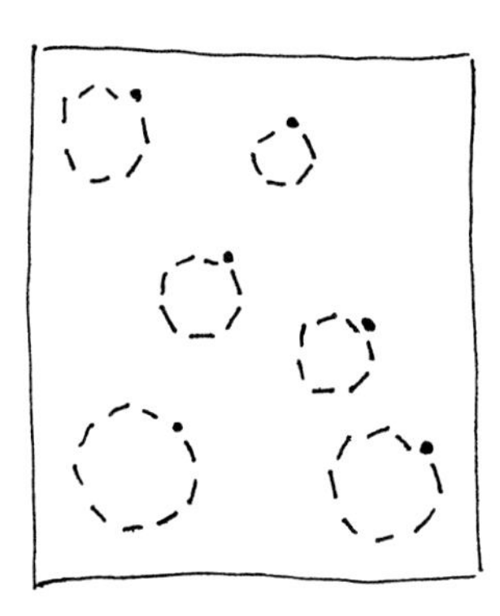

† Plain cotton or plain cotton/polyester. Use a cold water dye, and follow the instruction on the container.

Both gathered circles and lines of gathering worked on fine fabric† can be dyed with a similar result to tie and dye. Pull the gathers tight for dying. After dying is completed, allow the fabric to dry; then take out the gathering stitches, iron and admire.

Dolls and toys are often rather complicated, and bedevilled by gussets and seams, which, for some people, never come together in the right places. If a very simple shape is used instead, all these efforts can go into creating interesting features and decorations on the doll itself.

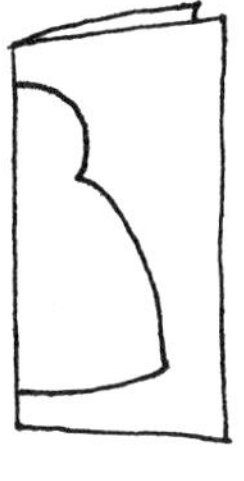

To make the pattern
Take a piece of paper and fold in half. Draw half the shape onto the paper, middle of the pattern to the fold. Cut around the shape and open out. This is the simple pattern. Try not to have any sharp corners.

Now transfer the pattern onto the background.* Have enough material for two patterns, a front and a back. The two sides need not be the same material.

* The easiest fabric to use for a doll is felt. However, wool or wool tweed are also easy, and cottons can also be used. Do not use fabric which is loosely woven or thin fabric which frays easily.

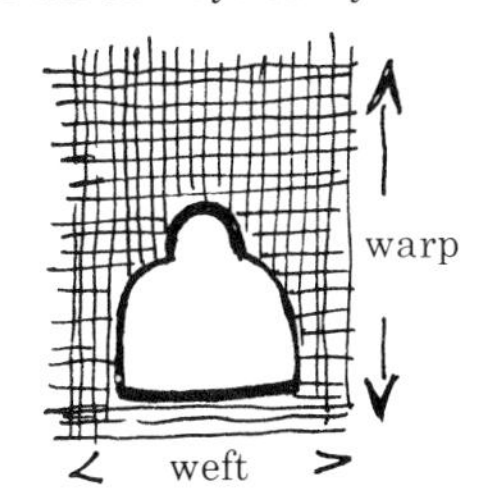

1 Place the pattern on the first piece of chosen material.**
2 Tack the pattern onto the material, and then make a line of running stitches on the background round the edge of the pattern. Use a thread which will show up on the background.
3 Remove the tackings and take off the paper pattern. The shape of the doll can then be seen in running stitches.

Now repeat stages 1, 2 and 3 on the other piece of material for the other side. There are now two sides with the shape in running stitch.
Do not cut out.

** It is important to make sure that the weft and warp of the material are running straight.
This will stop the fabric from pulling when it is sewn up.

44 First experiments making simple dolls. Boys and girls (7–9)

FABRIC AND THREAD

Now decorate the front and back of the doll shapes. Try to make both halves as interesting as possible, perhaps using some of the techniques described in the last few pages. When all the sewing and sticking has been done, cut round the shapes, leaving at least 2 cm for the seam. Take out the running stitches which marked the shape.

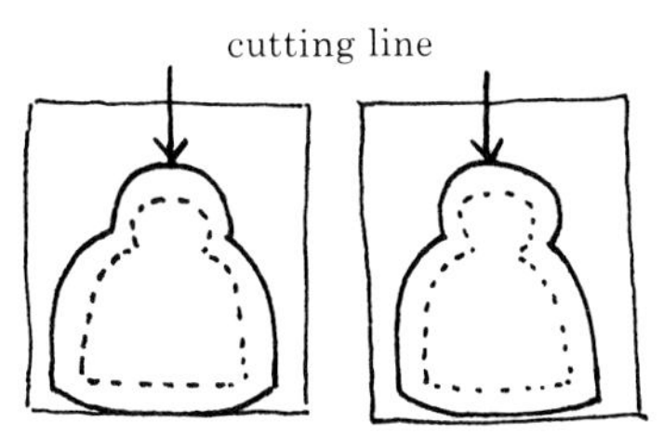

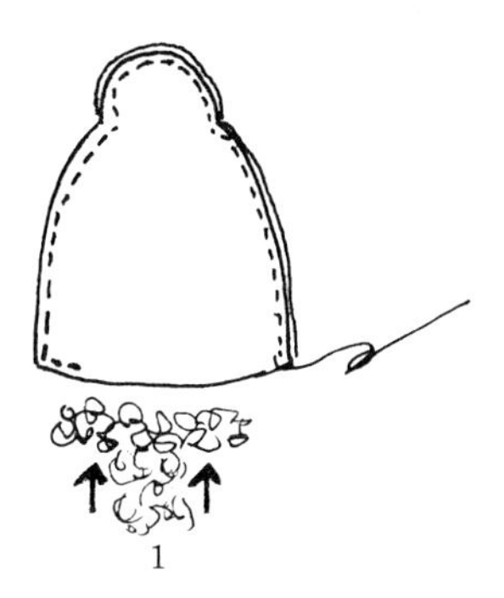

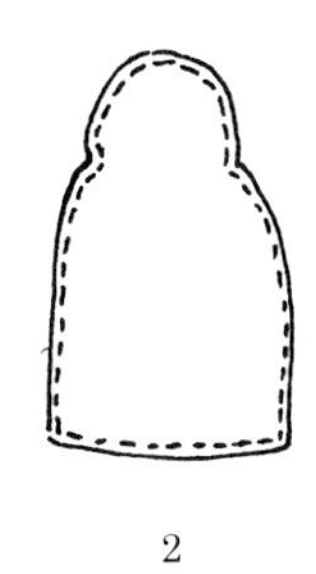

1 2

To join up

If felt or non-fraying material has been used, put both sides together, right sides facing out, and make a line of running stitches* right round the edge, about 2 cm in from the edge. Leave a slit across the base and then kapok** can be stuffed into the shape with a knitting needle (see 1). Stitch across the base (see 2). If cotton or a fabric which might fray has been used, put back and front right sides together. Tack round the edge, then back stitch round the edge. Take out the tacking. Turn the shape right side out and stuff (as in 1 and 2).

* Start with a knot. A knot is used to stop the thread from coming undone. It should be a reef knot. Hide it inside or at the back of the work. Two stitches to start off are not always strong enough. Use a knot where it doesn't show. If it does, as in transparent material, darn the end in where it shows least. To finish off, try to do two or three stitches then darn the end in at the back.

** Or shredded nylon tights.

Back stitch 1.

Back stitch 2.

Turn in a little fold or hem round the bottom. Close the slit with running stitch.

These dolls can be made in any simple shape. Try squares, circles, cones, etc.

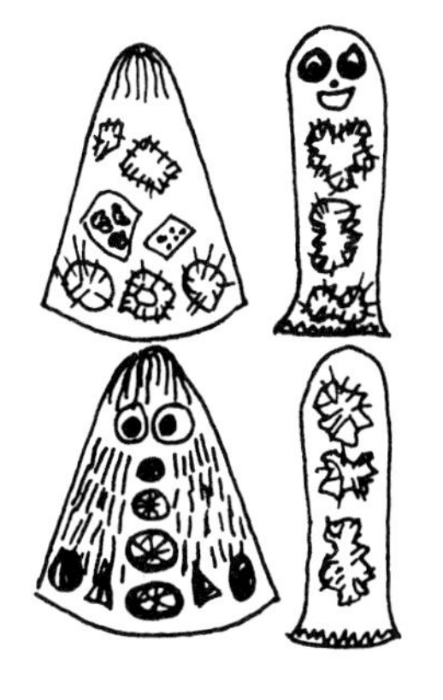

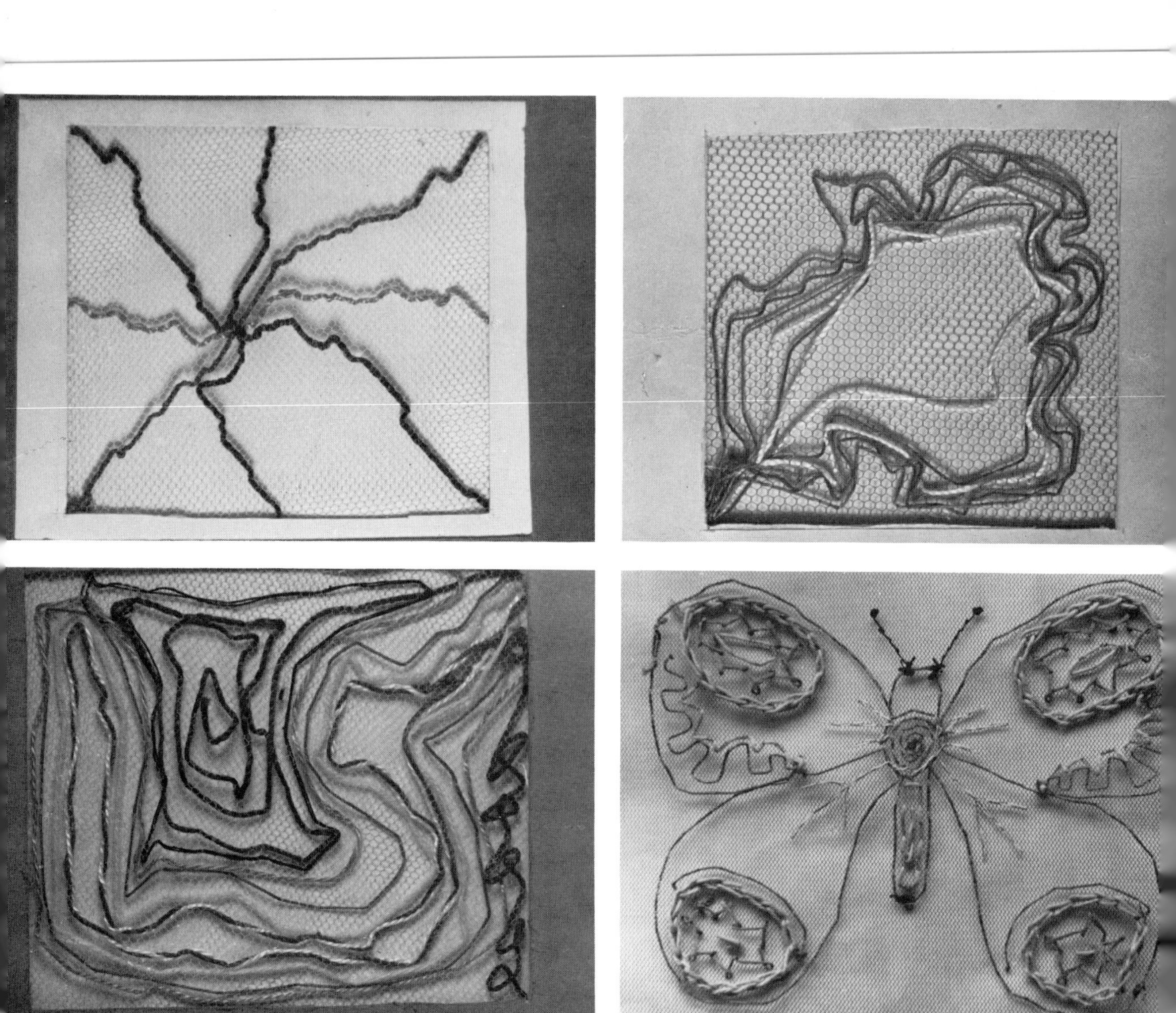

45–48 Making patterns on net. First experiments by Alison (10), Wendy (10), Janice (10) and butterfly by Alison (12)

Net

Net can be used like any other fabric in appliqué and collage, but it can also be used in one or two special ways, first because it has holes, and second because it is stiff and will not fray.

Making patterns on net

The net should be pinned onto a frame (see page 52), which makes it much easier to manage. Choose threads* which will pass through the holes easily. Make patterns by going in and out of the holes. Try different colours and weights of thread. Make linear patterns, curling, zigzagging and crossing. Try to make a picture. Decorate it with pattern. To begin, leave a thread which can later be woven in unobtrusively. Finish off in the same way. Motifs can be worked on a frame then cut out and applied to something else.

* Metallic thread, crochet cottons, stranded cotton using various numbers of strands, sewing cotton. Also wools and fine string.

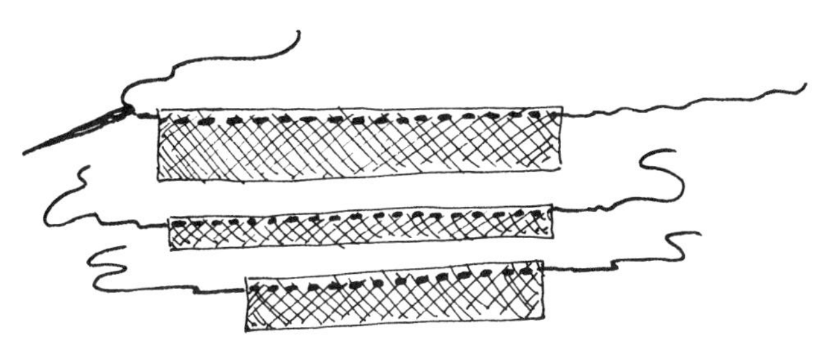

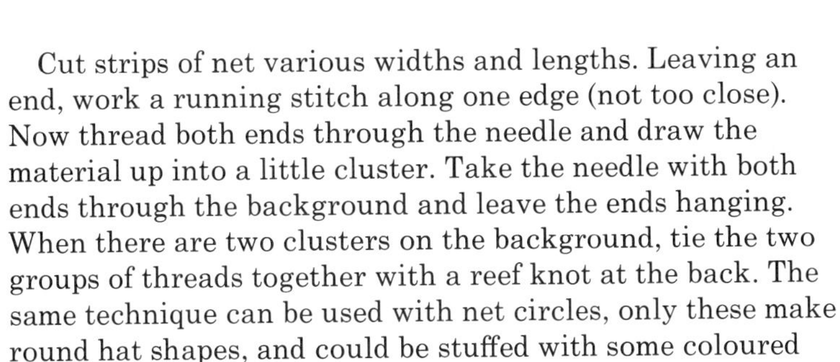

Cut strips of net various widths and lengths. Leaving an end, work a running stitch along one edge (not too close). Now thread both ends through the needle and draw the material up into a little cluster. Take the needle with both ends through the background and leave the ends hanging. When there are two clusters on the background, tie the two groups of threads together with a reef knot at the back. The same technique can be used with net circles, only these make round hat shapes, and could be stuffed with some coloured material or foil to shine through the holes.

Finish off at the back in the same way as the clusters. These net objects can be used to decorate a picture, or just by themselves as a pattern.

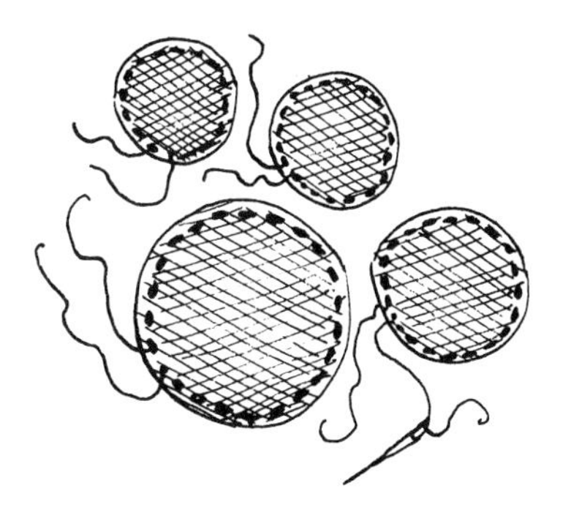

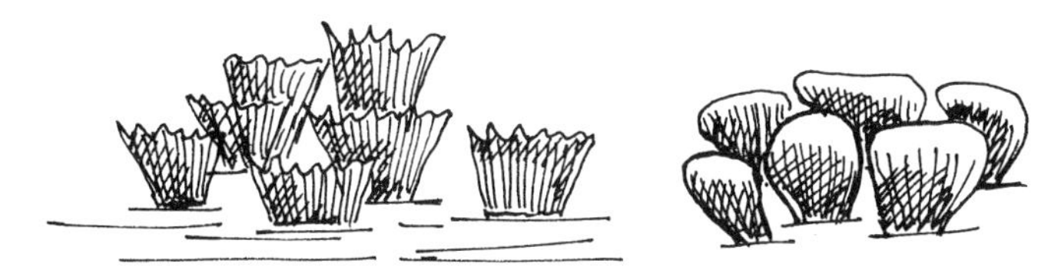

Organdie

This fabric is very fine and very strong. Pull it, to see how strong it is. Take some pieces of thread, and place them on a piece of white paper. Use coloured wool, white cotton, metallic thread, and stranded cotton. Now put a piece of organdie over the threads. You can see the threads through the translucent material, like shadows. Work done on organdie is called *shadow work.*

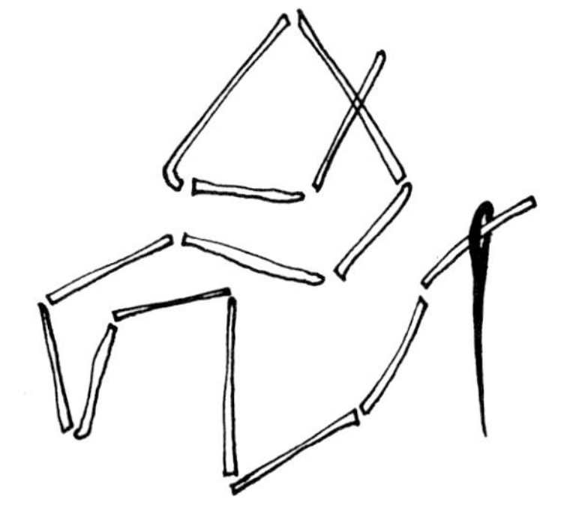

Using a sharp needle, and crochet cotton or wool, make straight stitches in the organdie. Only pick up the smallest piece of fabric with the needle, so that all the long stitches are on the upper side of the fabric and the tiny stitches are underneath. Turn over the fabric and look at the shadows of the stitches on the other side.

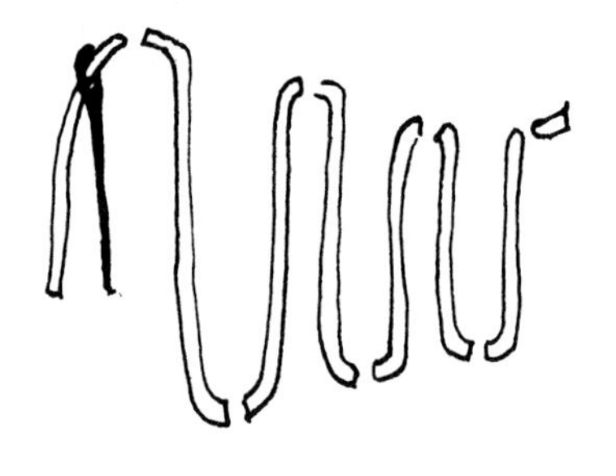

Try out different patterns. Try lines of stitches, and stitches going up and down. Try making stitches in circles and try making wheels, always keeping the long stitches at the same side. Don't pull too tight. Try to keep the material flat.

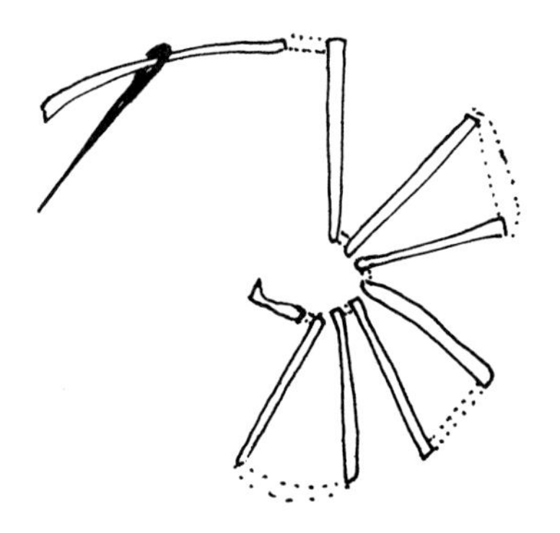

Use as many different threads as possible, trying out both thick and thin thread, and even both together. Try out different colours and black and white. See which looks most attractive. To start, leave the end of the thread hanging at the back. When the work is finished, weave it, and the end thread in and out of the stitches which have been worked. Try to do this so that it does not show.

Herringbone stitch can also be used in shadow work. In this stitch, most of the thread is on one side of the work. When the fabric is turned, the stitches can be seen through the translucent material.

The stitch is worked from left to right.

1 Take a small stitch at A. Take another small running stitch at B.

2 Go to C and take a small running stitch.

3 Go to D and take a small running stitch, etc. This working causes the thread to make a cross every time a stitch is taken. Try it out on organdie, and then turn the fabric and see the result. Try various threads for this, to see which is best.

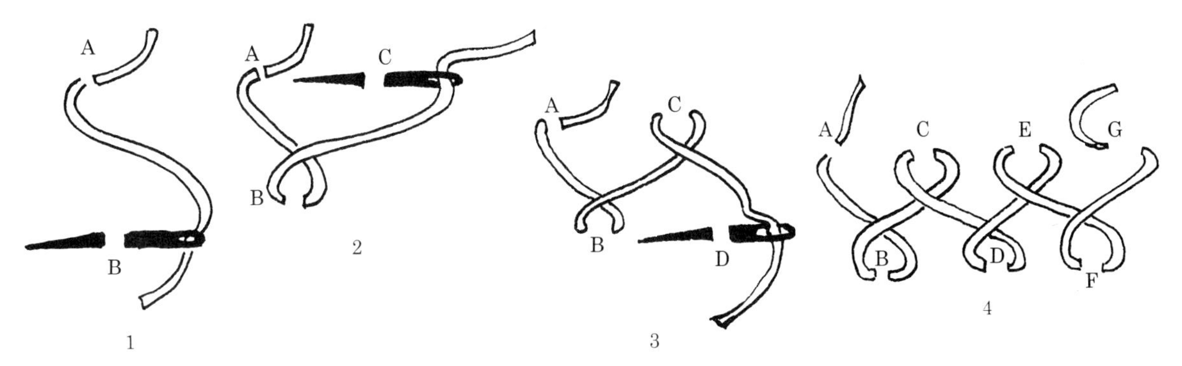

Another easy stitch to use in shadow work is laced running stitch.

Make a line of running stitches. Now take a different thread and lace it in and out of the running stitches. Don't pull it tight, but give the thread going in and out a good round shape. This stitch can be done in spirals and circles and zigzags. Try several. Use various threads. Also try out this work on any other translucent fabric which might be available.

Turn the work over to see the results.

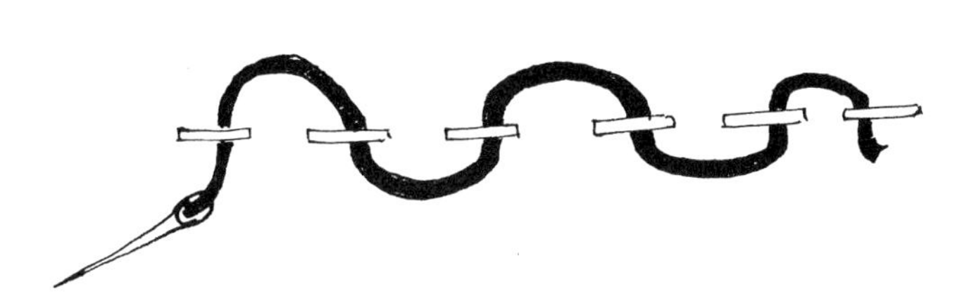

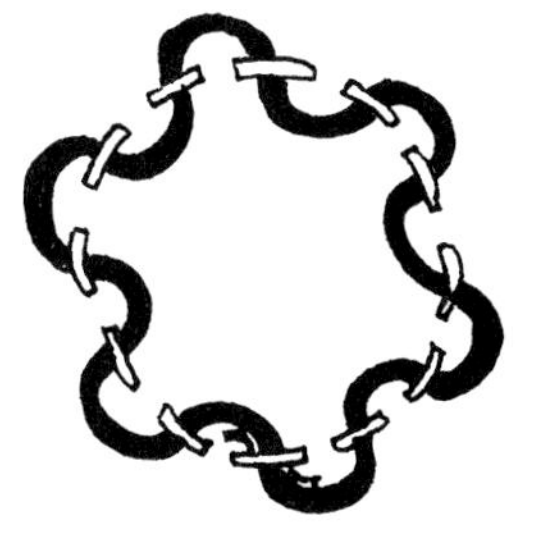

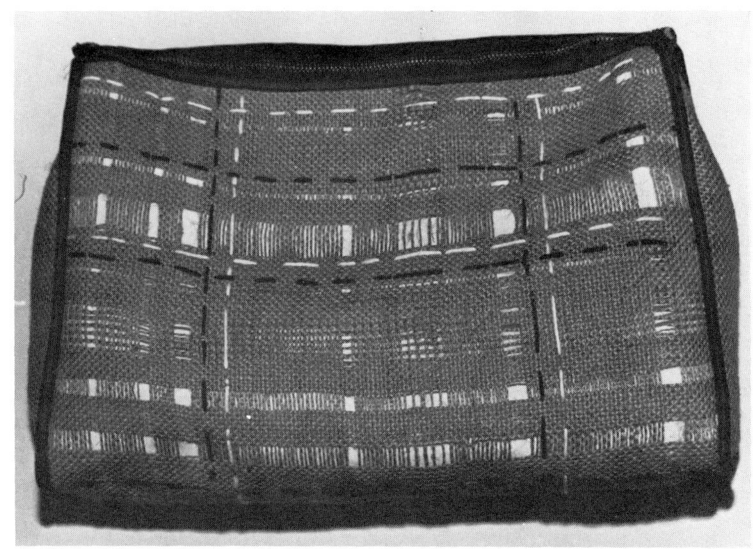

49 (above) Withdrawing and replacing threads (see page 75). Jason (10)
50 (below) Withdrawing and replacing warp and weft threads (see page 75). Girls (12–15)

Loose weave fabric

Try out some of the threads in your collection by weaving in and out of the holes in some loose weave fabric.* It is not necessary to use a needle at this stage. Some loose weave fabrics, like sacking or scrim, are so loose that they need to be machined round the edge with a zigzag stitch to hold them firm.

* Fancy net curtaining, garden net, mesh vegetable bags, wide mesh dishcloths, sacking and scrims. Plastic net is easiest to start with.

See page 35 for home made threads.

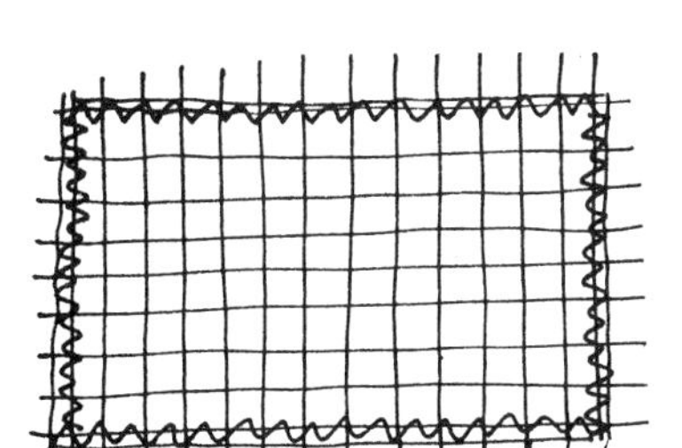

Use a good variety of thread, both thick and thin. Try very thick threads, which bulge out of the background and try weaving plaits and braids into the background. Use a strip of net, pulling it up into puffs every time it comes to the surface of the background fabric. Experiment with as many threads as possible: leather, angora wool, braid, nylon tights with knots, ric-rac braid, net strip, raffene, corduroy strip, nylon knit strip, plaited string.

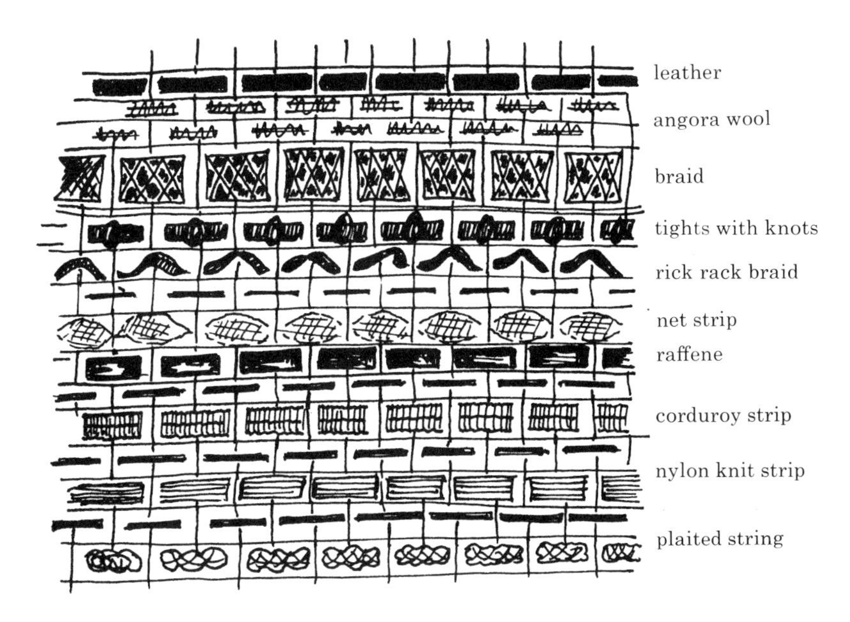

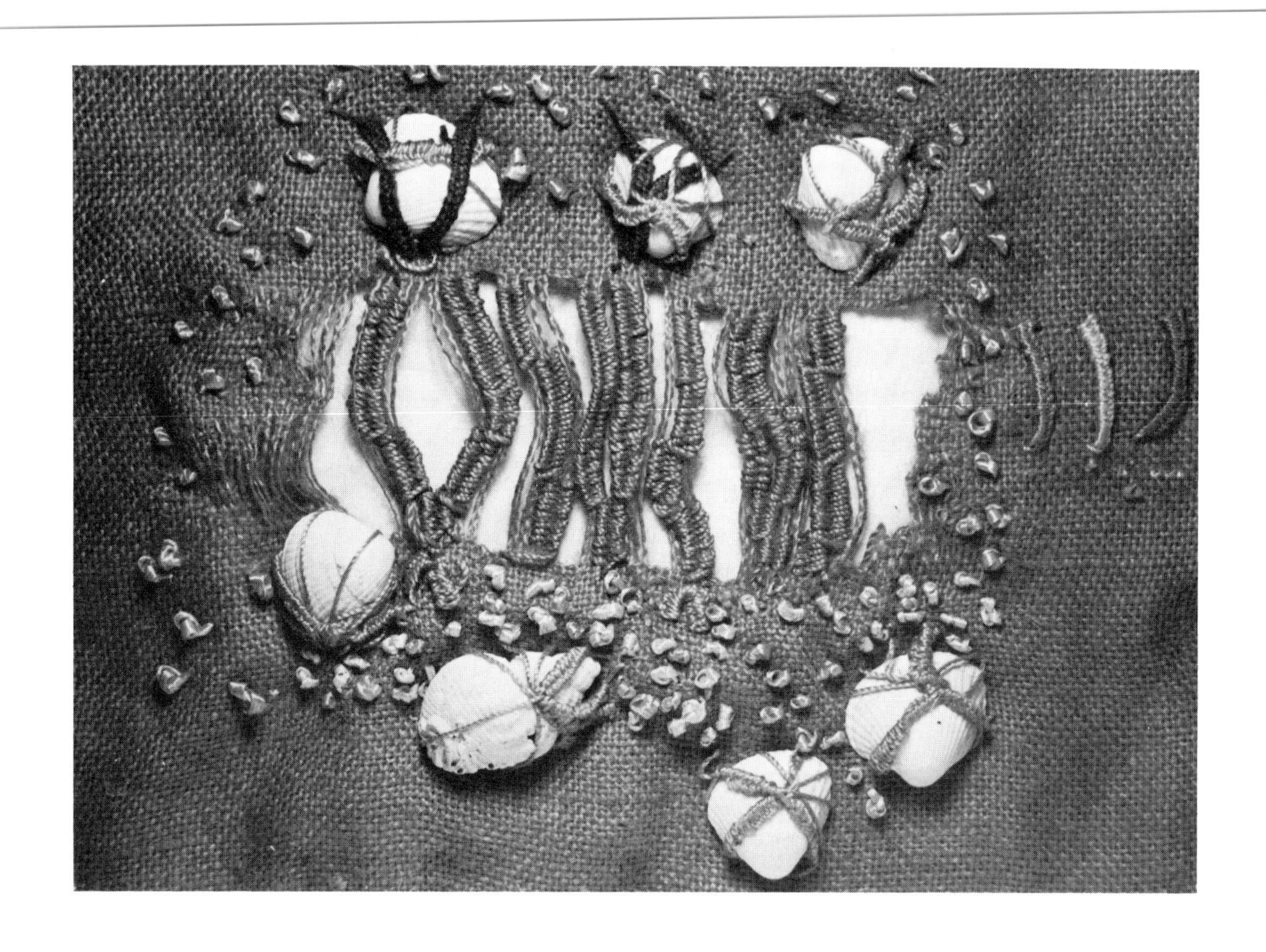

51 Withdrawing threads and needleweaving (see page 75). Note: needleweaving on threads holding shells. John (10)

Using a loose weave* fabric, pull some of the weft threads right out of the material. Look at the patterns which are made. See the effect of pulling out a lot of threads, and just a few. Experiment with different fabrics, to see which ones are easiest to take to pieces.

* This must be loose woven. Try hessian, scrim, various tweeds, sackcloth, some loose weave curtaining.
It is sometimes easier to pull the threads from the middle to the sides, as this does not disturb the side warps so much.

Next, pull both weft and warp threads to see the effect.
Now choose some threads and weave them in and out of the holes made by the withdrawn threads, as on the previous page. Try various colours and experiment with home-made threads, plaits, braids and ribbons.

Another idea is to group the threads in bundles** using a backstitch. Weave both ends of the thread into the work afterwards.

** See also page 67 for backstitch.

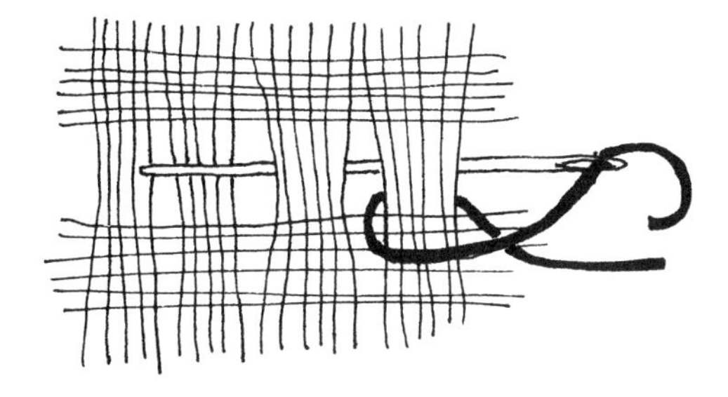

Backstitch 1

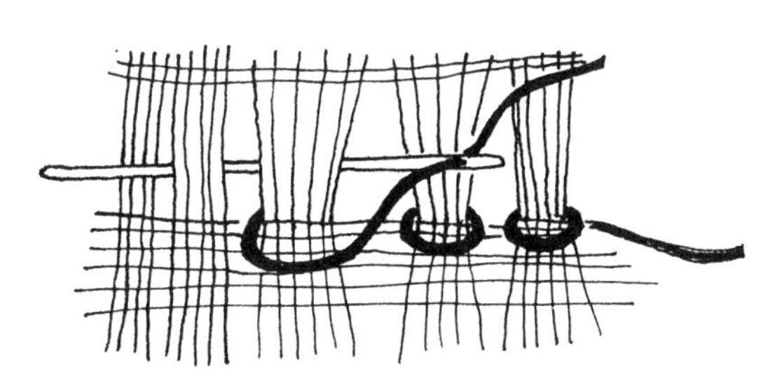

Backstitch 2.

It is interesting to try some needleweaving in and out of the warps left when the threads are withdrawn.

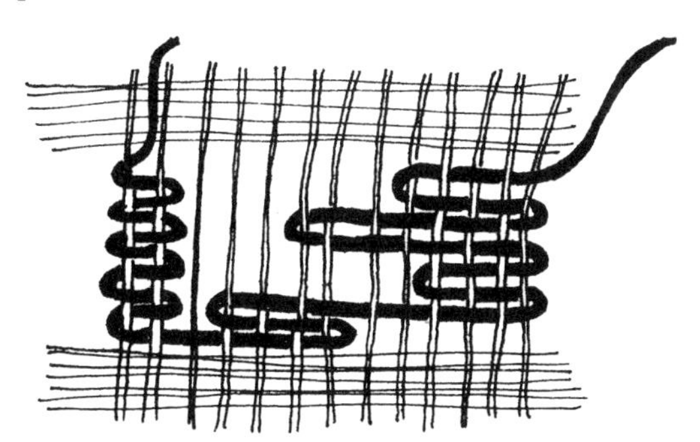

Choose a very loose woven fabric.* With the fingers, part the fabric to make a hole without damaging or removing the threads.

* Sacking, carpet wrappings, bandage and gauze, some curtaining, various types of scrim.

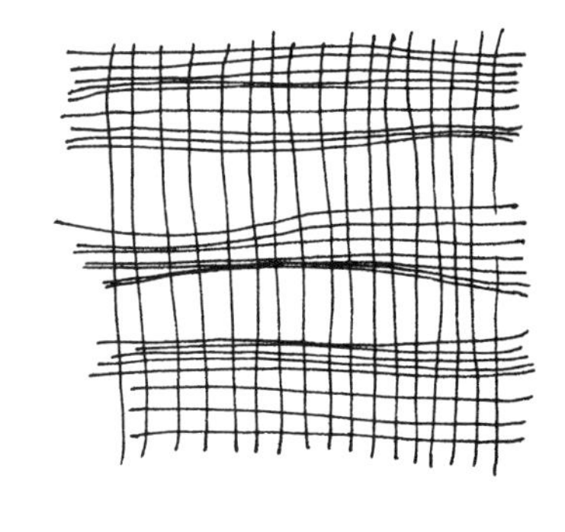

Find different ways of parting the fabric, making rows of holes, patterns and 'roads'. Push the threads around to see how they react.

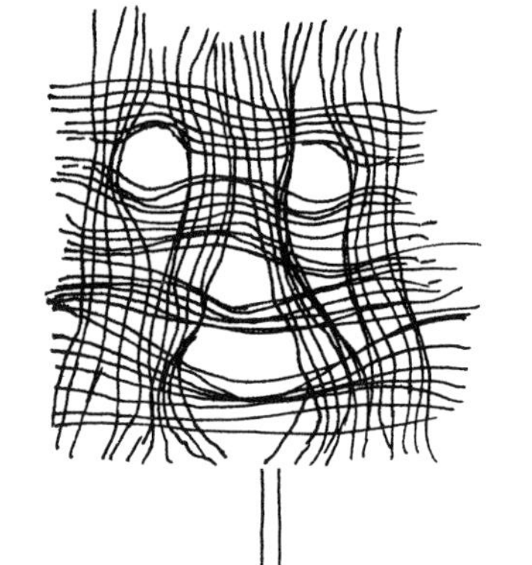

Try to make a face in the fabric, for a mask. Take care not to tear the fabric or remove threads.

Now try the effect of the holey fabric over various other materials, using coloured, plain textures, shiny, and patterned backgrounds, to see which looks best.

The holes which can be pulled in loose weave fabric close up again, but it is possible to keep them open with stitches. Use a loose weave fabric and a rounded needle and some strong thread.*

* *Coton-à-broder*, several strands of embroidery cotton, crochet cotton, vest cotton.

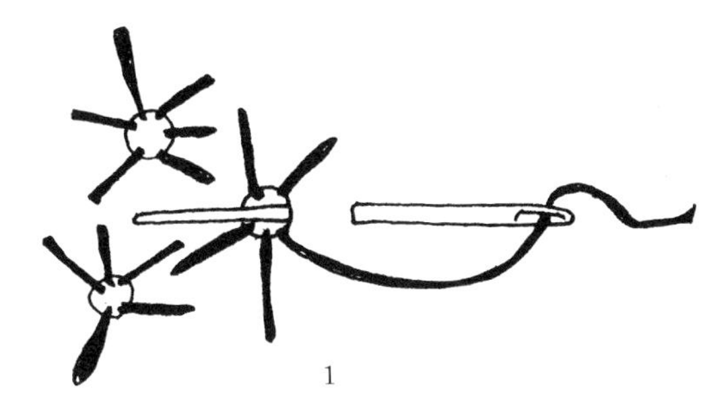

1

Use *satin stitch*. This is a back stitch which moves down every stitch, winding the thread round the fabric and holding it in place. A knot would slip through the fabric, so keep a longish end and weave in afterwards. Try** to make stars (see 1) with the stitch, pulling tight so that the stitches pull the fabric into holes. Make the stars different sizes, some close and some spaced out. Try them the same size in rows. Make different numbers of points. Experiment with colours and threads. When one star is finished, take the thread to the back and make several stitches to hold the star in place, then go onto the next, without breaking the thread.

** This sort of work is easier to do on a frame, which will prevent distortion.

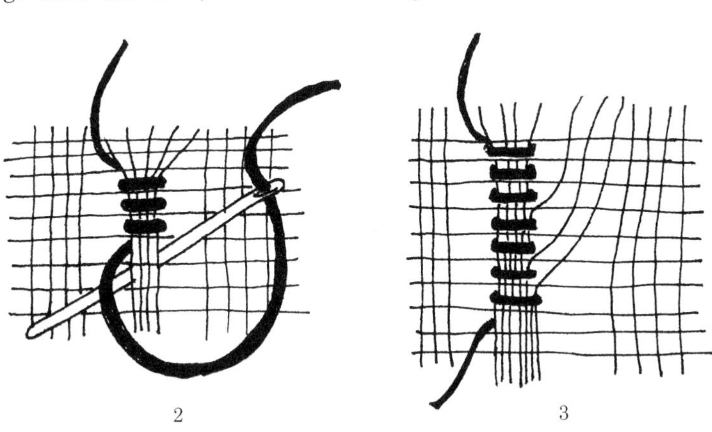

2 3

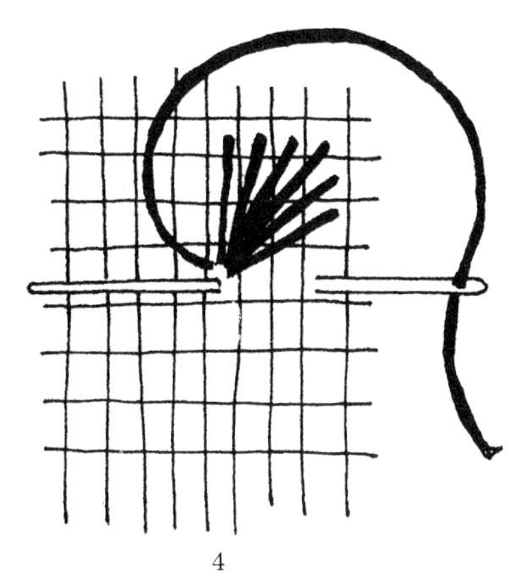

4

Try to make 'roads' or lines (see 2) on the fabric with the satin stitches. Go over several threads, or just two or three. Experiment with variations in tension.

Make lines which gradually gather in more threads (see 3). Make patterns with lines worked both vertically and horizontally. Vary the number of threads.

Make a star over three threads (see 4). Work right round the square. Try a half square or just a quarter.

Try out both even and uneven patterns.

Needleweaving

Weaving is usually done on some sort of a loom, but it can also be done on fabric. It is then called *needleweaving*. To do successful needleweaving, the background has to be kept taut, so that the warp threads do not wrinkle the material. Therefore it is usually done on a frame.* However, needleweaving can also be done on a piece of stiffened** material.

First, the warp threads are sewn onto the background. The only time the needle goes through the background is when the warp threads are sewn in. The weaving is done on the warp threads.

Using a sharp, strong needle thread a length of strong thread (button thread, crochet cotton) and tie a knot about 4 cm from the end.

Starting at the back of the material, bring the thread up onto the surface. Go back, having made a long stitch. Come up again, and make another stitch, and continue in the same way until several long stitches have been made. Take the thread to the back, and tie the end to the end left below the knot. Tie a firm reef knot. It is important that these stitches or warps are taut and firm.

* Using a frame. See page 52.

** A background can be made by pasting (cellulose or wallpaper paste) a piece of material onto the smooth side of a piece of corrugated card. The card is just thin enough to pierce with a needle, but strong enough to keep the material taut. Leave to dry thoroughly or cover a round of polystyrene with material and use as a base.

Cut a piece of material a little bigger than the polystyrene shape. Take a running stitch near the edge (not too near). Pull and envelop the polystyrene. Start with a knot and finish firmly with several stitches. Now cut a circle of felt a little smaller than the shape. Stick onto the bottom to neaten. Leave to dry thoroughly.

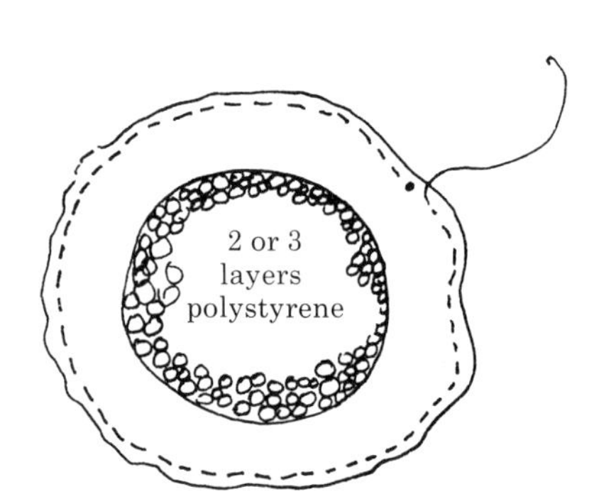

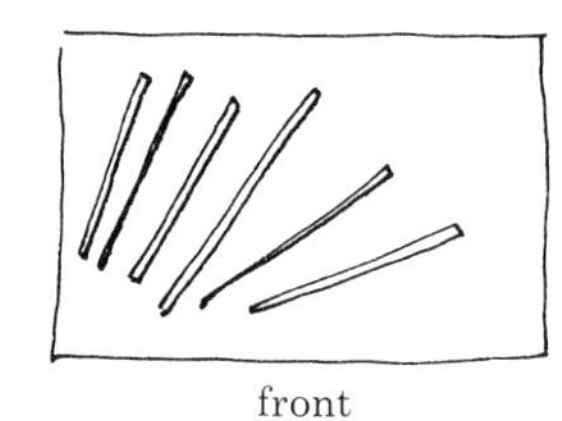

front

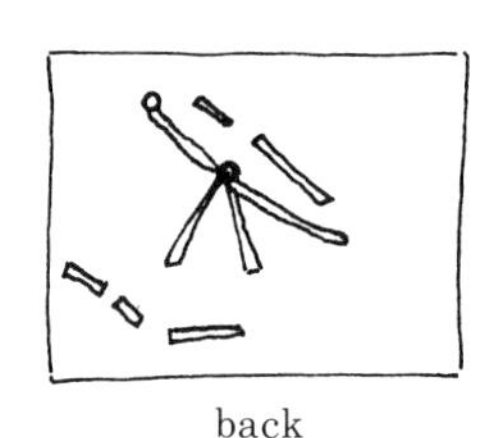

back

Now that the warp threads have been prepared (see 1), the needleweaving is done on these stitches (see 2).

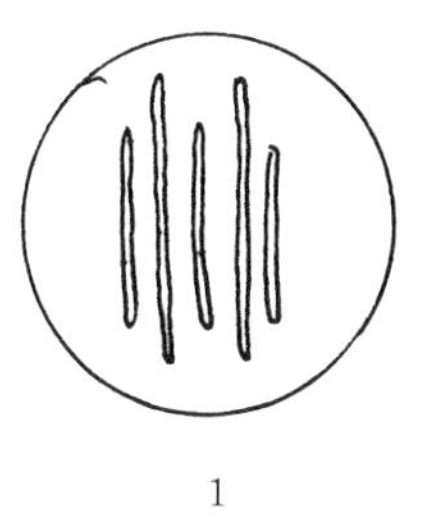

1

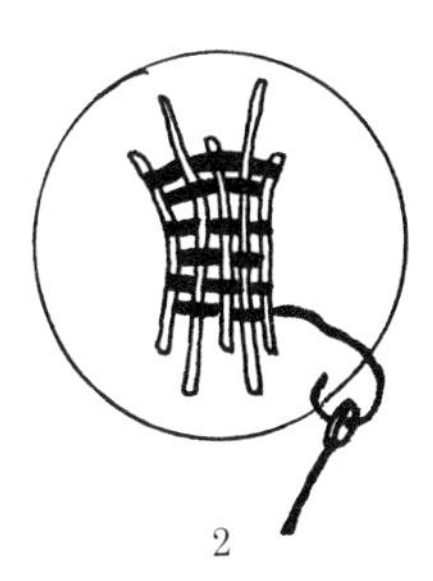

2

Use a blunt needle and bring the weaving threads from the back of the work, behind the warp stitches. Weave in and out of the warp stitches. To change colour, or at the end of a thread, push the needle back into the background under cover of the weaving, so that it does not show, or slide the needle between the weavings for a little way and cut off.

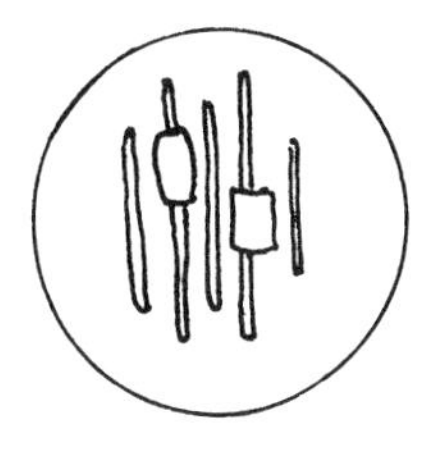

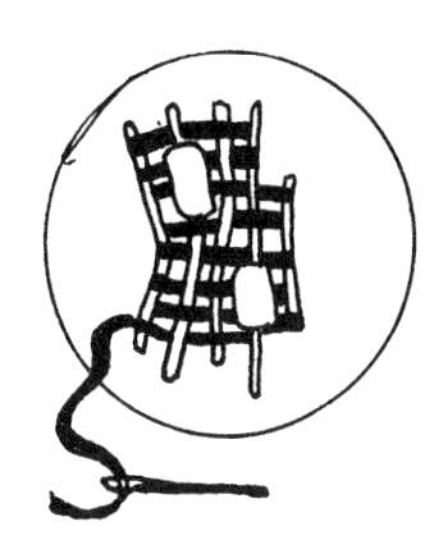

When preparing the warp stitches, beads can be threaded onto some of them and then the needleweaving is worked round them. Try out different threads,* and different textures** for needleweaving. It does not matter if the warp stitches are left uncovered, and if the colour of the warp stitches is chosen to fit in with the colour of the background and the needleweaving threads, so much the better.

* Needleweaving is very successful when carried out in threads which have been dyed together, or in threads which have all been chosen to match in colour.

** Try threads with slubs, and try weaving yarns, and metallic threads.

Experiment with the positions of the warp threads. Try them in different patterns. Make the needleweavings jump from one lot of warps to the next.

Needleweaving is effective when the work is superimposed one over another.

1 Work over three, four or five warp threads.

2 Lay another group of warp stitches over the first and work these.

3 Lay a third group and work these. Try these experiments at different angles and with different threads. Try dark colours working up to light, and tones of the same colour.

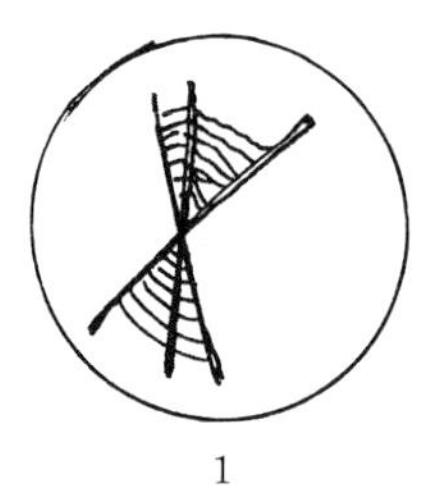

Here, only two warps at a time have been used. Lay and weave two warps, then superimpose two more warps, and weave. Continue to do this until a really textured effect has been achieved.

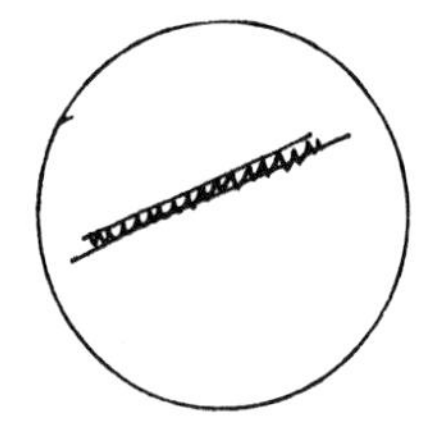

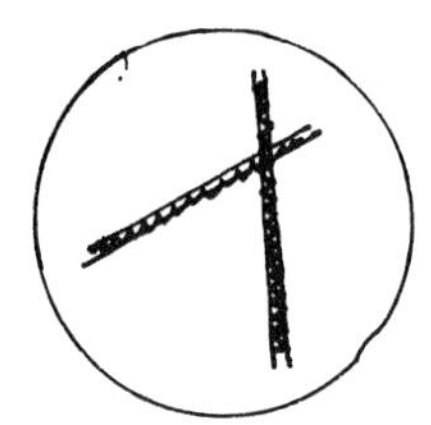

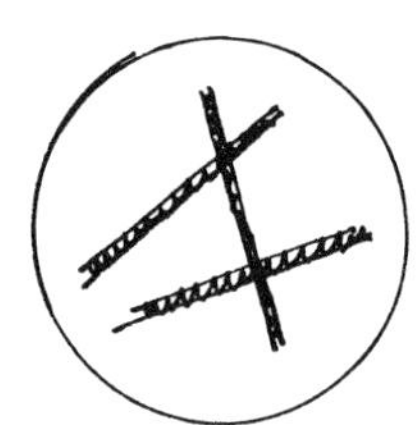

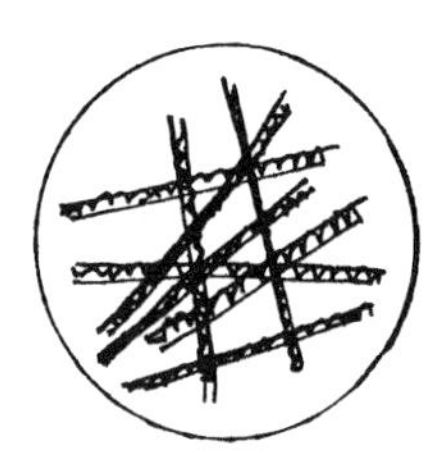

To give a really three-dimensional effect, bring the warp stitches up through the middle of a wooden bead. This raises the warps above the background. Buttons, covered cotton reels, stones with holes, or even a piece of felt or covered polystyrene with a hole in the middle can be used. Also try using the rolled shapes in Section 1 page 19.

Bead seen from above.

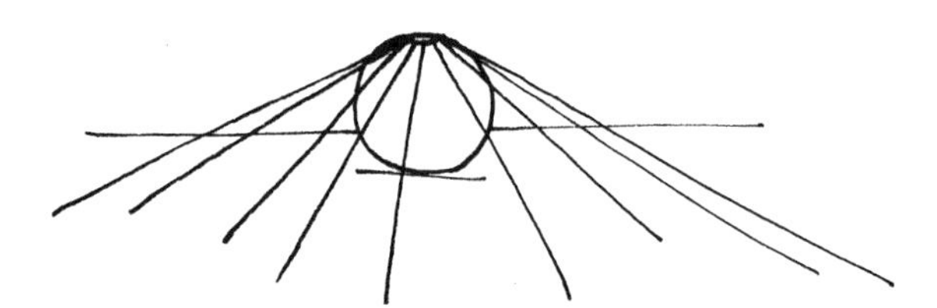

Bring the weaving thread up through the hole in the bead, and weave round and round the warp threads over the bead. Make sure there is an odd number of warp threads for this. To change colour or to finish off, slide the needle behind the weaving and back into the hole, or slide the needle through the background, by the bead. It is not necessary completely to cover all the warp threads. Another and very attractive way of weaving over a bead is only slightly more complicated, and well worth learning.

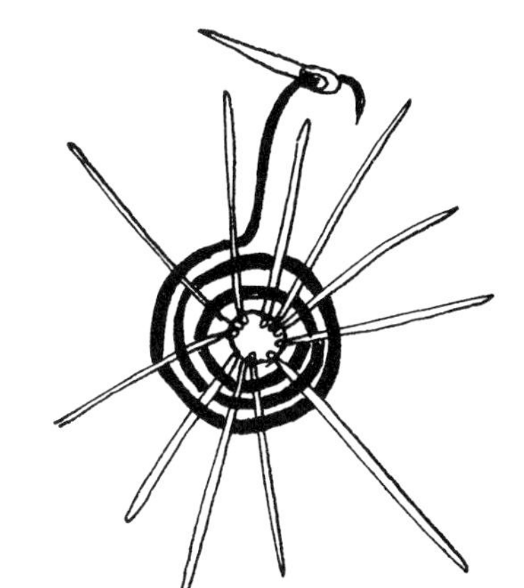

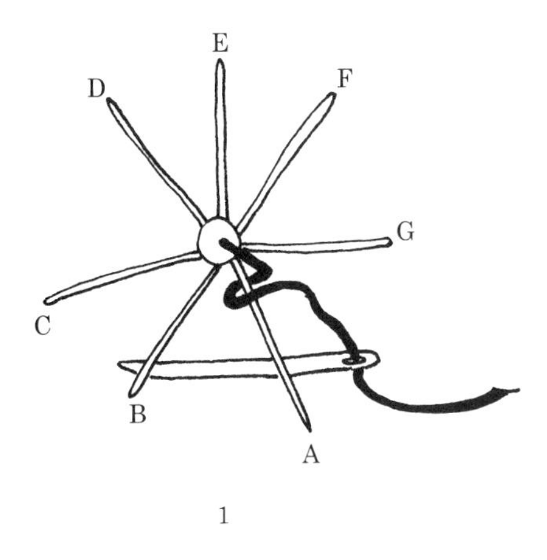

1

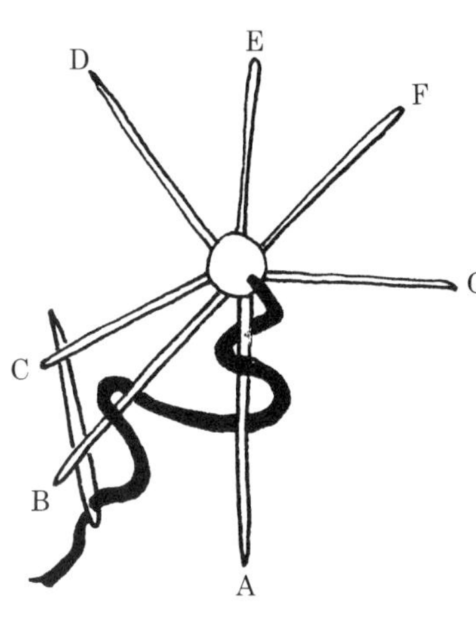

2

1 Bring the needle through the hole in the bead. Take it under thread A then over thread A. Take it under thread A and thread B.
2 Take the thread back over thread B then take under thread B and thread C.

Continue, taking the needle over thread C and under thread C and thread D. Then over thread D and under thread D and thread E, etc. For this, it does not matter how many warp threads there are. These spiders webs can be done without beads, and they are very effective in groups.

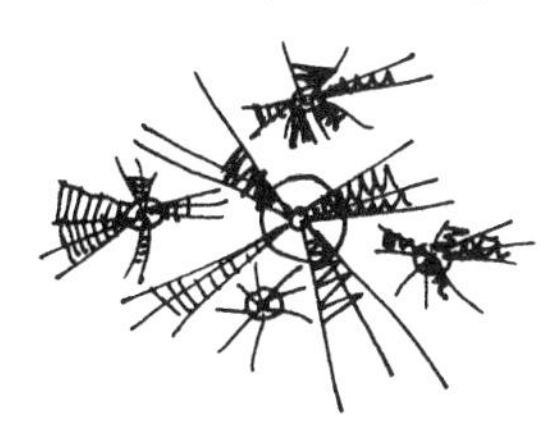

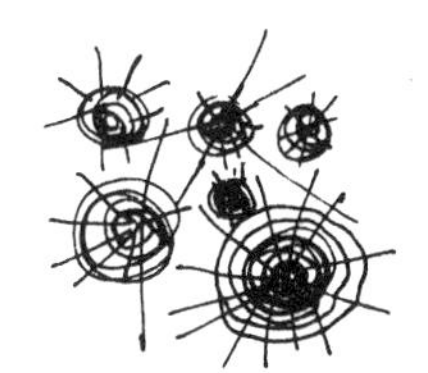

Beads

Make a collection of beads.* Discuss why they are used and what they are made of.** Look out for beads from other countries, and pictures of people wearing beads. Look at beads spread out on various fabrics, like velvet, satin, tweed, leather, fabric with metallic threads, nets, taffeta, etc. See what sorts of beads look best with each background.

Beads kept in cardboard boxes can easily be spilled, so they can be stored in glass or plastic jars,† with screw top lids, sorted into colours. To look at them more closely, pour into a cardboard lid with a rim. Pour back into their container through a funnel. Beads can be made by hand from paper.

* Old jewellery, jumble sales, craft shops, Indian and far eastern craft shops.

** Try to look at glass beads, cut-glass beads, plastic beads, china beads, wooden beads, large and tiny beads.

† Empty spice jars, baby food jars, coffee jars.

Paper beads
Take a strip of paper about 30 cm long and 2 cm wide. Fold lengthwise. Cut a long triangle on folded edge, gradually widening to one end (see 1). Dip the triangle of paper into cellulose paste, then wind round a knitting needle as gently and as evenly as possible (see 3 and 4). Do not wind too tightly, so that the bead will slide easily off the needle. Stand on end to dry.

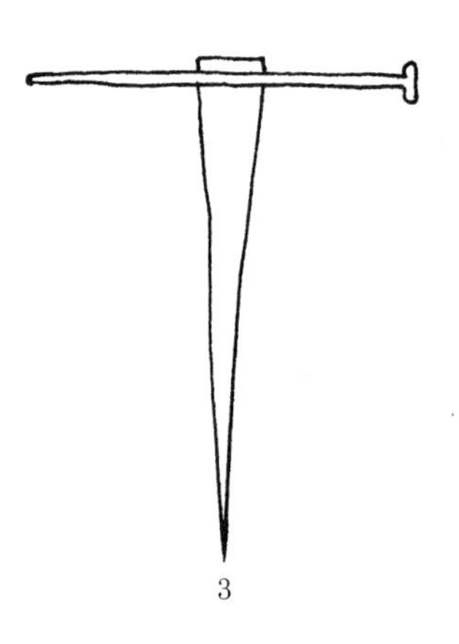

3

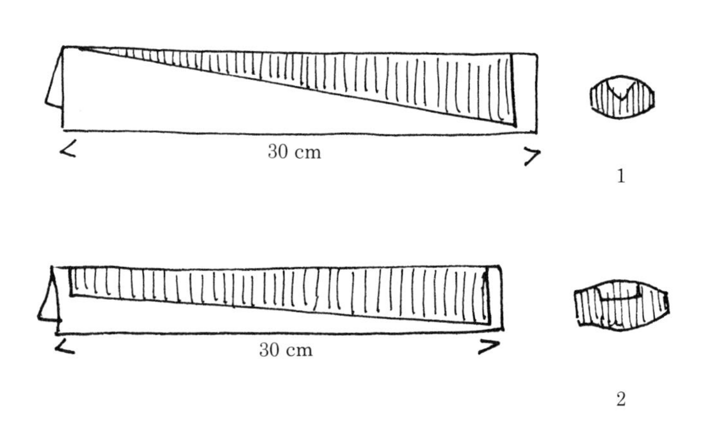

1

2

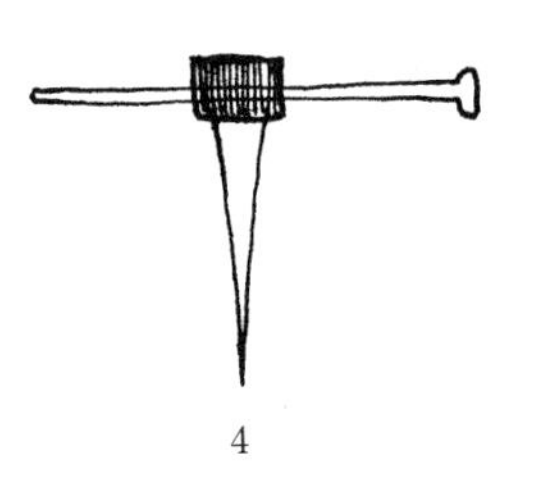

4

These beads can be made from wallpaper, thin coloured card, tissue paper, wrapping paper. To make small beads, reduce width and length. The triangular shape makes rounded beads, a long rectangle makes squared beads. Choose paper with patterns and stripes to make more interesting beads. Leave to dry hard for two or three days, then paint and varnish if necessary.

Interesting beads can be made in the same way as paper beads, by rolling strips of leather, vinyl, suede or silver foil round a knitting needle. Glue along one side and roll round a knitting needle, but leave a space at the beginning, without glue, so that the material does not stick to the knitting needle. Clay beads of various sizes and shapes can be made both using clay which does not need firing, and ordinary clay which can be fired in a kiln. Make sure the clay is worked well, to prevent cracks. Beads can be made from sections of drinking straws, bamboo cane, some hollow stalks, washers and bolts, empty cotton reels, covered with fabric (try strips of corduroy) or painted. Dowels can be sawn into sections and a hole drilled down the middle.

Always be on the look-out for other things which might be used as beads in ironmongers shops, in do-it-yourself shops, and even in supermarkets.

52 Beads made from clay, fringed vinyl, wallpaper, silver paper, wrapping paper, straws, rolled leather, rolled vinyl. Caroline (12) and Philippa (14)

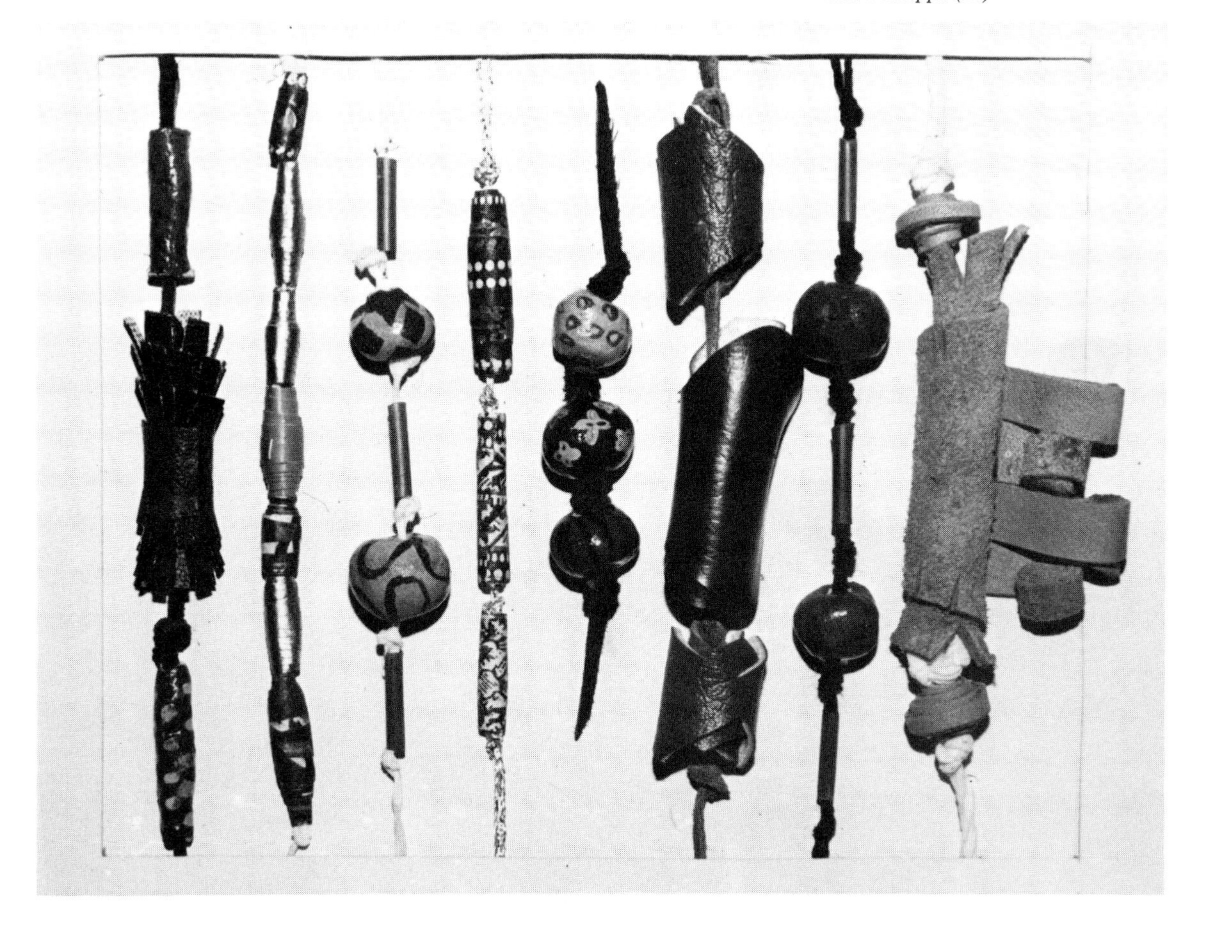

Pompons

Pompons are balls made of wool, which can be used as decoration in three-dimensional work, and also to decorate weavings.

1 Take two circles of card,* both the same size. The size of the circle will be the size of the finished pompon. Cut a smaller circle in the middle of each. Put the circles one on top of the other.

2 Wind thread round and round the two circles, until the card is covered and the inner circle almost closed. Use plenty of thread as the finished pompon should be fat and bouncy.

3 With sharp scissors, cut through the threads round the edge of the circles (see 4).

4 Part the two cards slightly (see 5 for side view). Tie** a strong thread round the wool between the cards.

5 Take away the card circles. They can be cut or pulled off. If they are pulled off the circles can be used again.

Pompons can be made in two or three colours by using different coloured threads. Mix both threads and colours.

* Circles must be accurate. Draw round something or use a pair of compasses.

** Use a reef knot.

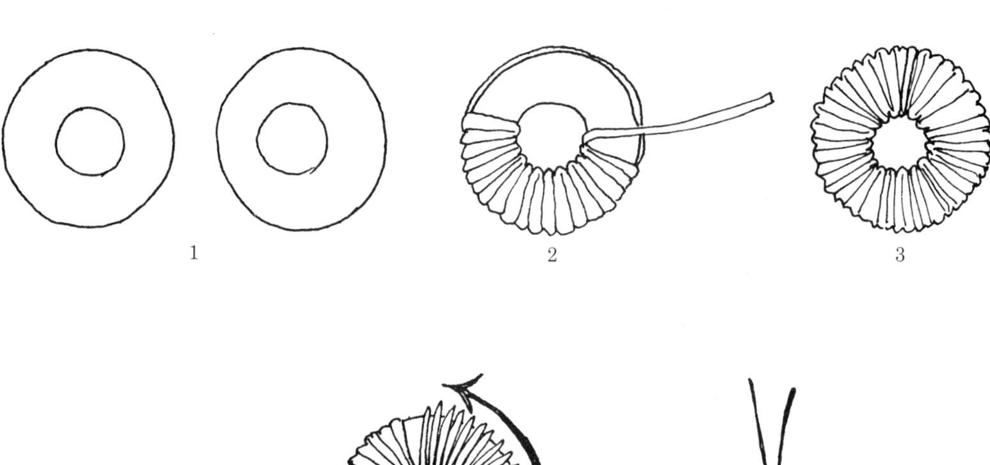

1 2 3

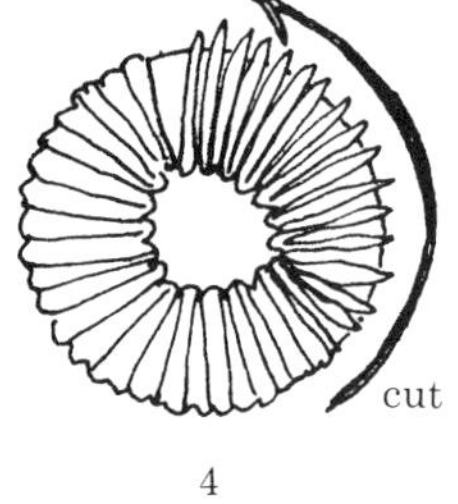

4

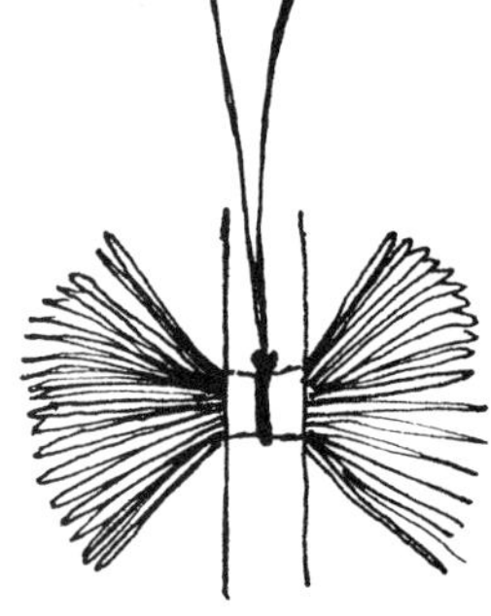

5

Covered rings

It is sometimes desirable to cover a ring* with thread, to make it fit into a scheme of work. This is easily done by working a series of half hitches over the ring, with a needle and thread. This is, in fact, *blanket* or *buttonhole* stitch. When the ring is finished, fix it onto the background with the two end threads.

* Curtain rings. Rings made from wire. Rings made from a thread wound round the end of the finger.

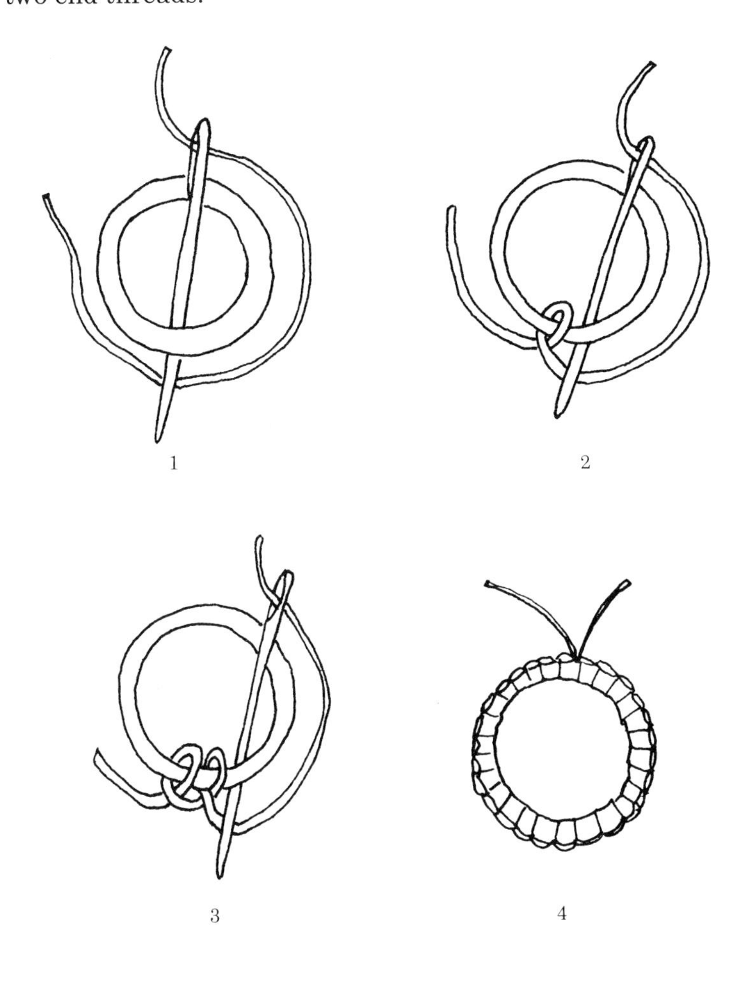

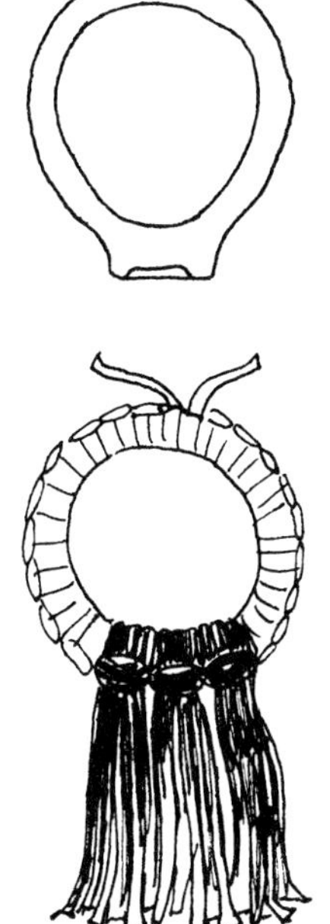

Any thread may be used for this work, and weaving yarns with slubs, threads made from nylon tights, ribbons, and string may be used, as well as wool and cotton. This technique can be used to cover such diverse things as beer can tops,** wire netting and bundles of wire, which might then be incorporated into a piece of work. It is always worth experimenting with new ideas.

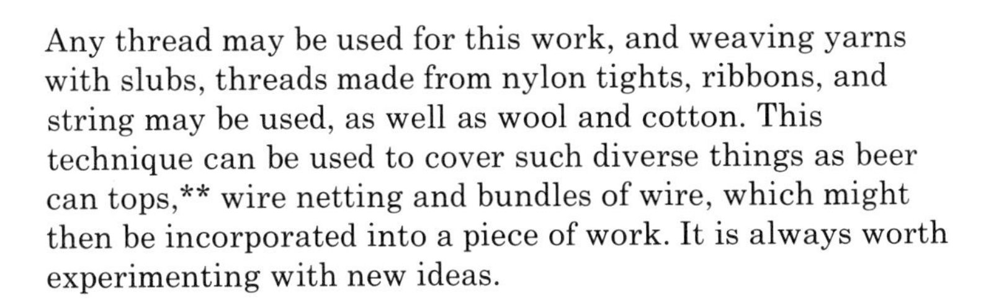

** Beer can top.

Beer can top covered plus fringe.

Fringes

* Try wool, tweed, hessian, cotton, rayon, furnishing fabric.

** Use runing stitch or back stitch.

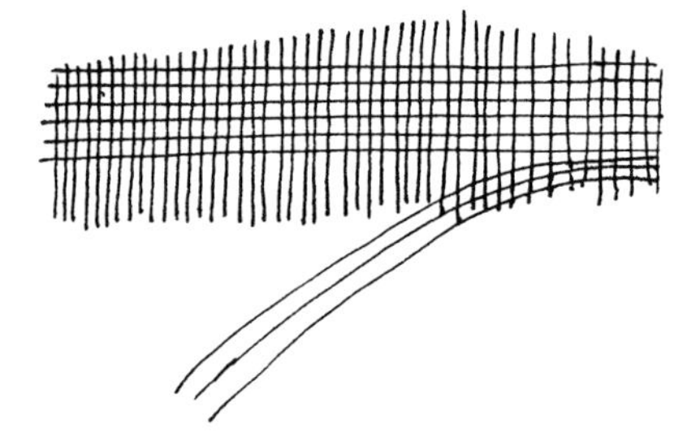

Find as many different woven materials* as possible. Take out threads alone one edge, so that a fringe is formed. Now take out some threads at the edge which is at right angles to the first. Are these threads different? One set is weft threads, and the other set is warp threads. Which are most attractive? Compare the fringes made by different woven materials. Now, put the two together to make a double fringe. Choose fringes which go well together. Try fringes in the same colour, but made from different fabric. Try several fringes of different lengths superimposed. Stick them along the top, or stitch together.**

It may be possible to plait or braid some of the fringes. Try this. Tie a knot at the bottom to stop the braids from coming out.

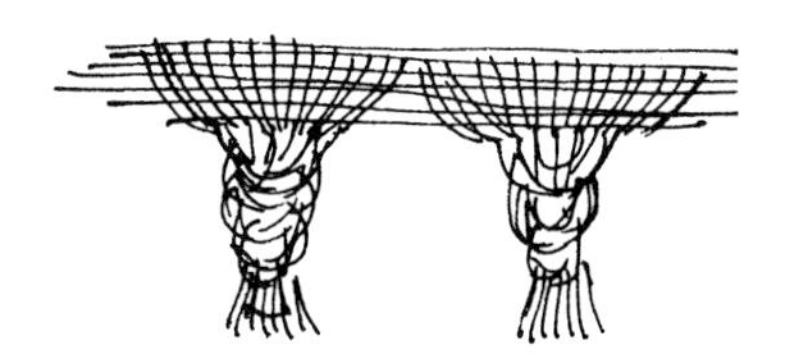

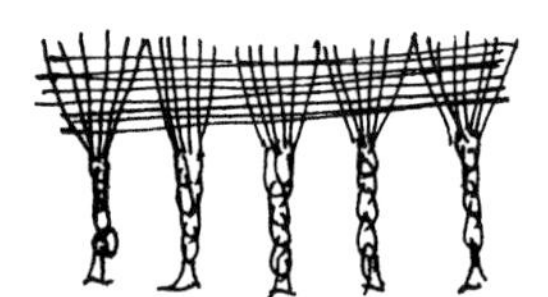

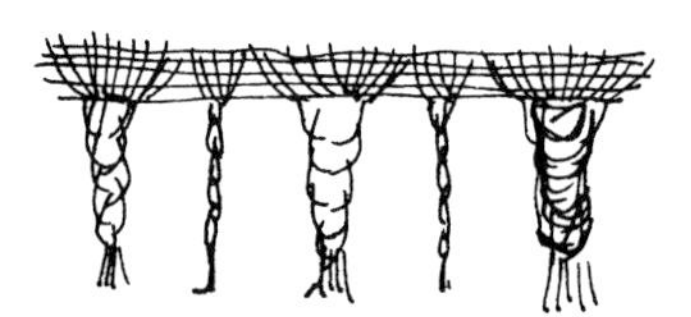

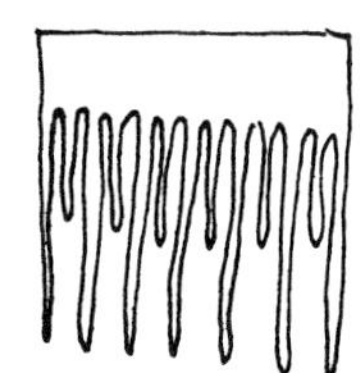

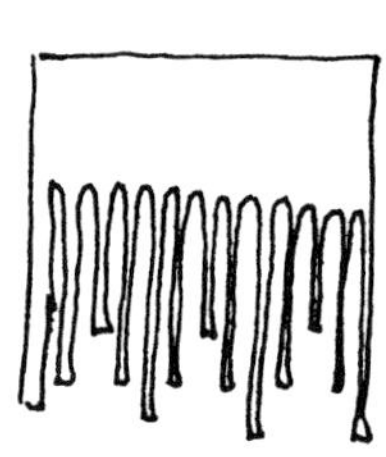

† All jersey fabrics, felt, leather, suede, vinyl.

Using a non-woven fabric,† a fringe can be made by carefully cutting from the edge up into the fabric in thin strips. This takes some practise and sharp scissors. Start off by cutting narrow fringes, gradually working up to a long fringe. Make interesting fringes by superimposing a narrow fringe onto a long fringe. Use these cut fringes with the fringes made from woven fabric. It is also possible to cut the bottom of a non-woven fringe in patterns or layers.

To add a fringe to the bottom of a piece of work, or a piece of material, either through punched holes, or through fabric:

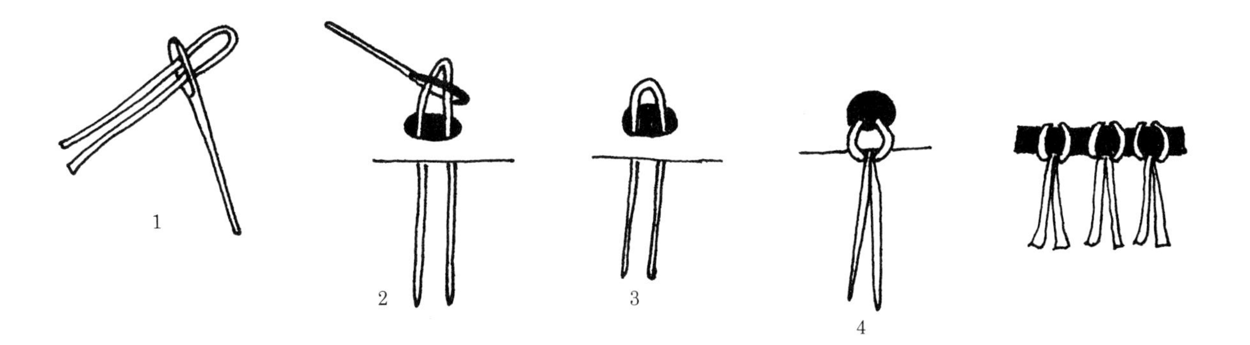

1 Take a thread, fold in half, thread the loop through a needle.
2 From the back, take the needle through the hole (or fabric) with the loop only. Leave the ends hanging down (see 2 and 3).
3 Unthread needle.*
4 Take the two ends of thread, put through loop and pull down. A line of these will make a fringe.
5 These lark's head knots can be worked over a strip of leather, a piece of string, or any thread, to make a fringe. Try this using several threads instead of one.

* Use a needle with a big eye. Alternatively, use a crochet hook, if available, to pull the loop through the hole, or the fabric.

Using the three methods described, fringes can be made out of almost any type of fabric and thread. Experiment with different types of fabric and thread and use different colours. Use fringes of various sorts together.

The top of a fringe can be decorated by sewing, or sticking a braid or cord (see pages 88–92) along the top of the fringe.

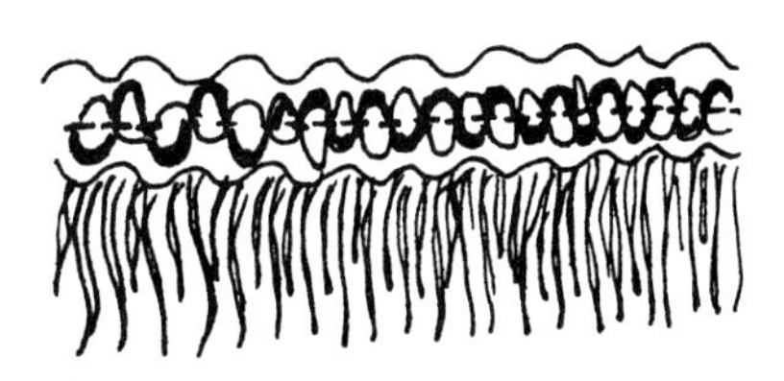
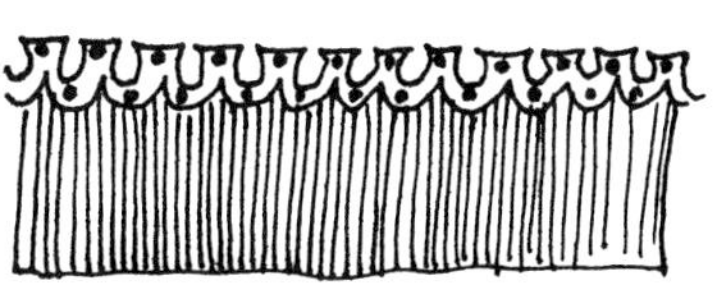
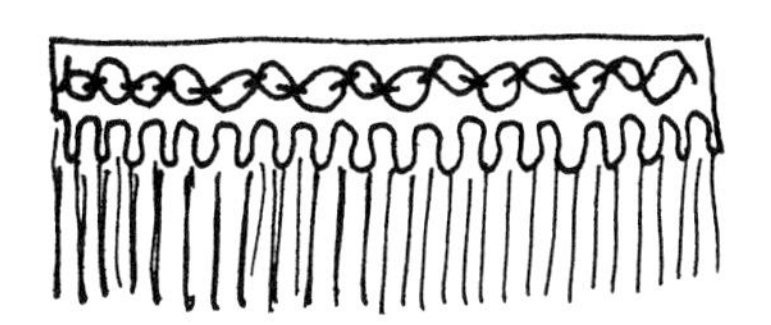

Making braids, plaits and cords

* This can take two people. It is also possible to thread scissors onto the cord, or hang a weight on the cord. These will slide down to the middle and weight the cord down, so that it twists onto itself more evenly. Cut scissors free and tie a knot at the cut end.

*1 Twisted cord**

Take several strands of thread, twice as long as the desired cord. Tie a knot at each end and pin one end to a suitable place with a drawing pin. Slide a stick through the other end. Twist the stick until all the threads are twisted together. When they are so tight that they begin to distort, put the two ends together, while holding the middle of the twisted threads with the other hand. Remove pin and stick. Now let the two sides twist together to make a thick cord. Try this with different colours, different thicknesses of thread. Use strips of material, suede and leather, ribbon, as well as wool, metallic thread, silks and cotton, etc.

2 Finger cord using one thread

Practise this cord using string before trying other threads. Follow the diagrams. Make a running noose (or a loop which can be made bigger or smaller by pulling the end. See diagrams 1–4.)

Put a loop of string through the running loop. Tighten (see 5).

Continue putting a loop through the running loop until the cord is the desired length. Finish off by putting the end of the string through the loop. This is important to stop the cord from unravelling.

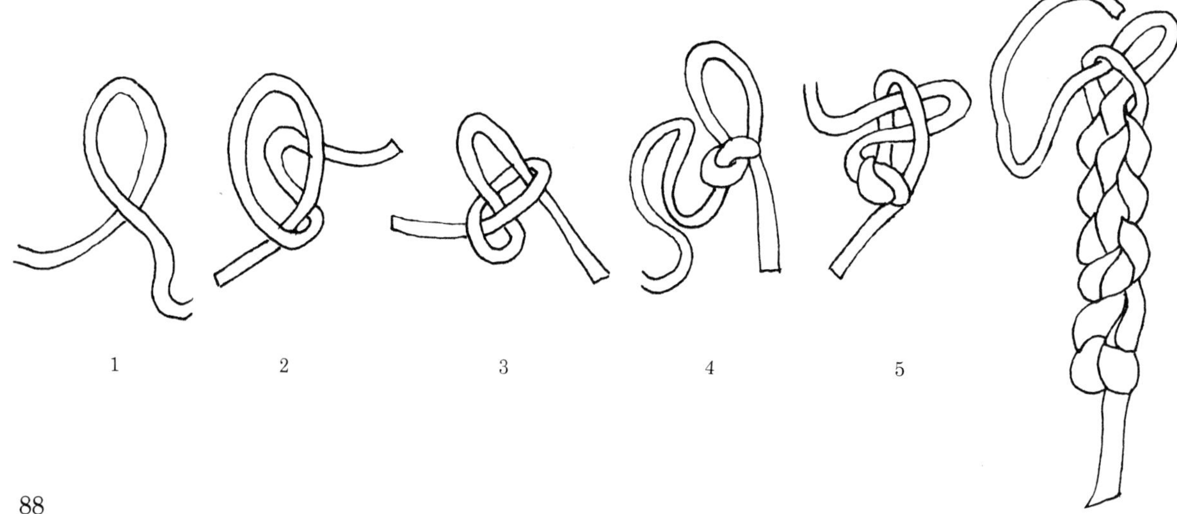

3 Finger cord using two threads
Practise with two different colours. Tie the two threads together.

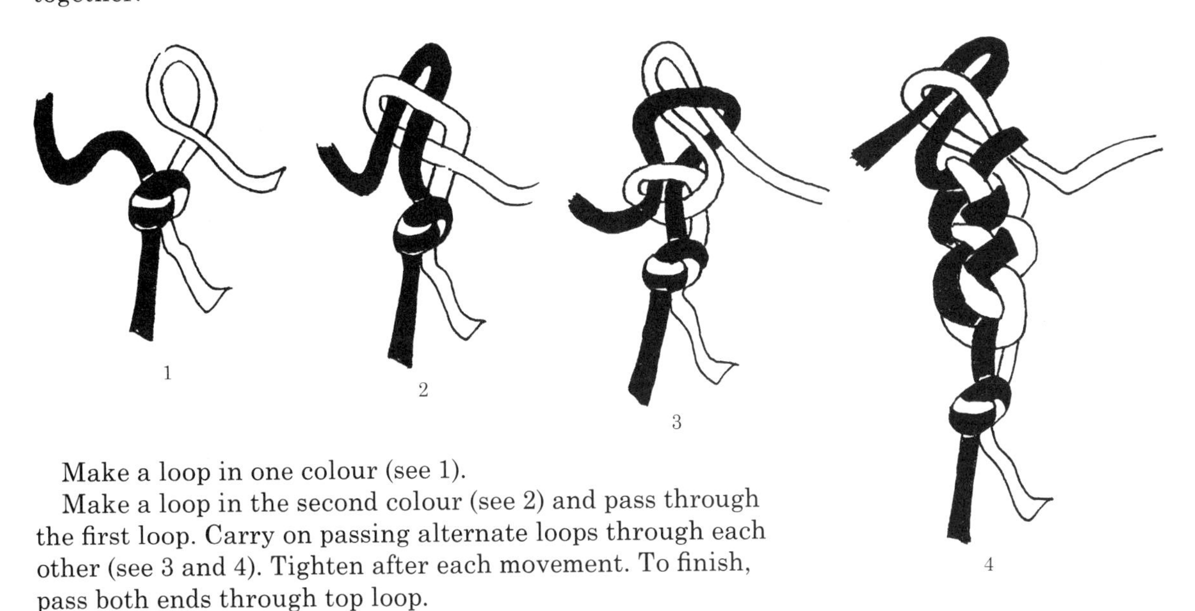

Make a loop in one colour (see 1).

Make a loop in the second colour (see 2) and pass through the first loop. Carry on passing alternate loops through each other (see 3 and 4). Tighten after each movement. To finish, pass both ends through top loop.

4 Finger cord using three threads
This is usually called a plait. Practise in three different colours.

The alternate outside threads are brought into the middle. Start by knotting all three ends together. Finish in the same way. It is sometimes easier to attach the top of the plait to a block of wood, or a board while working. Plaits can be made from any sort of thread, mixed threads, several threads together, and are also effective made from strips of fabric, suede, felt, ribbon, nylon stockings, etc.

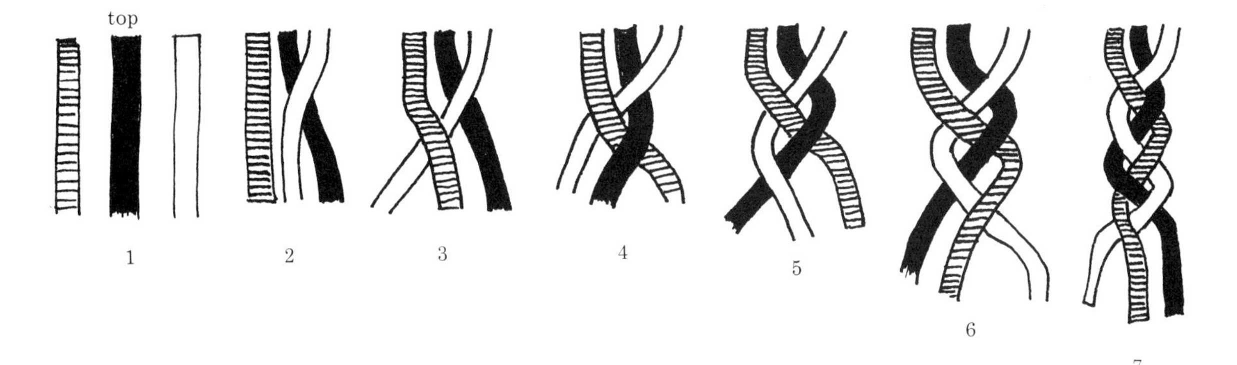

5 Finger cord using four threads

This cord has been drawn in four colours for clarity, but it looks best worked in just two colours, the two left threads in one colour, the two right threads in another colour.

Follow the diagrams carefully. Start and finish with a knot. The outside right thread is brought behind two threads, and back over the second (see 2 and 3). The outside left thread is brought behind the two threads next to it (see 4) and back over the second (see 5). The outside right thread is again brought behind two threads (see 6) and back over one (see 7). The outside left thread is also brought behind two threads (see 8) and back over one, and so on.

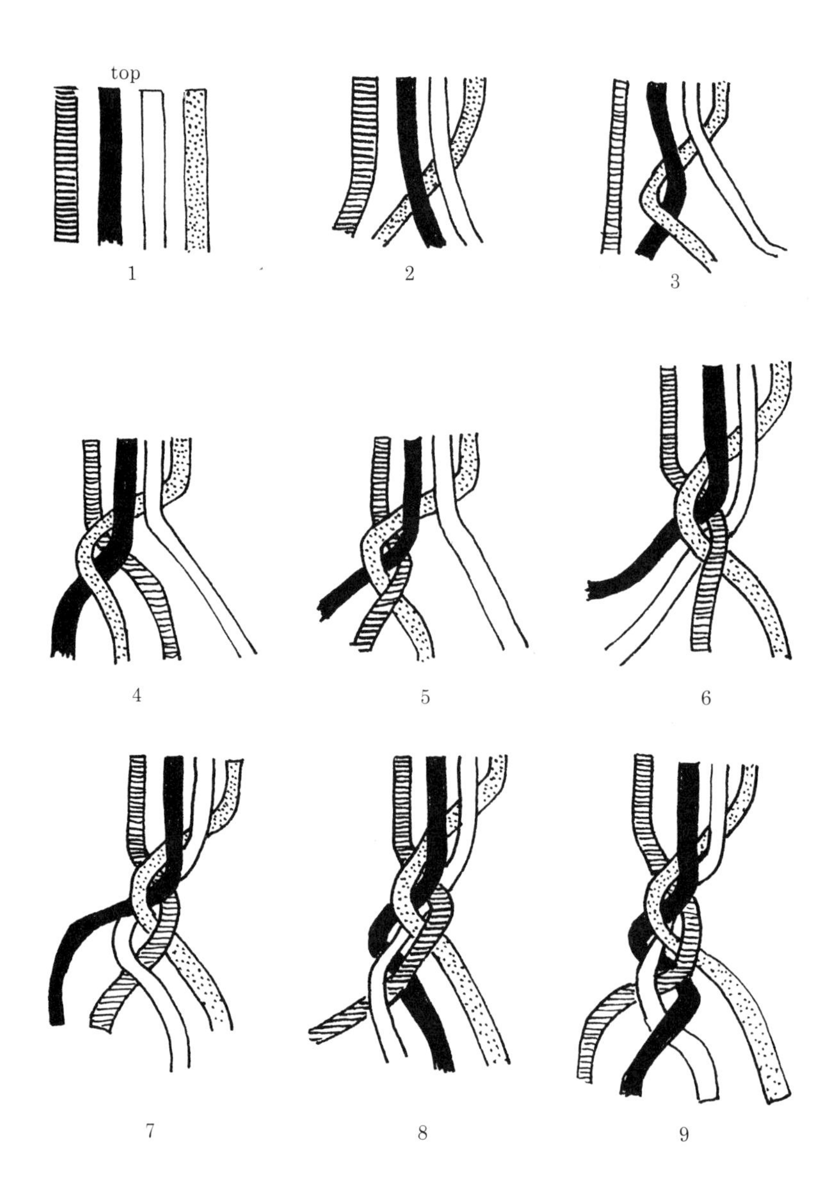

6 Knotted braid using two threads
Practise this with two pieces of string. It is easier if the threads are fixed at the top to hold them steady. Pin them with a drawing pin, or tie to the back of a chair. One string is knotted onto the other string in a line of half hitches. As the cord progresses it will twist of its own accord. Try it out using other threads.*

* Include metallic thread, macramé string, cotton, jute and hemp string, wool, rug wool, etc.

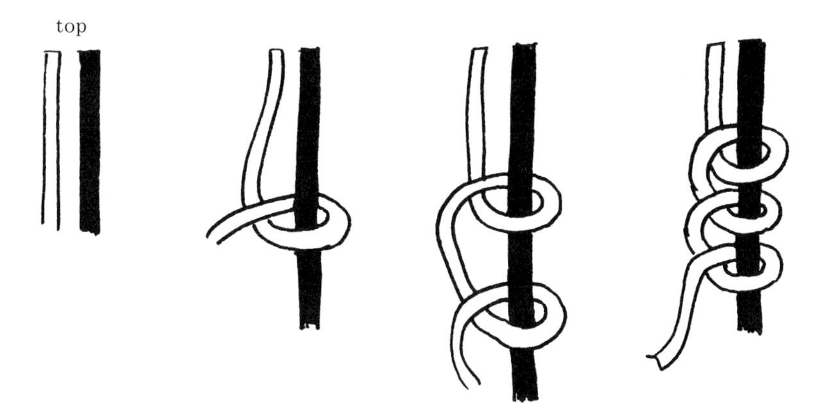

7 Knotted braid using two threads
Practise, if possible, with two different colours. The left thread is knotted onto the right thread with a half hitch. The right thread is then knotted onto the left thread with a half hitch, and so on.

This makes a flat cord. Again, always experiment with different threads, and different weights of thread used together.

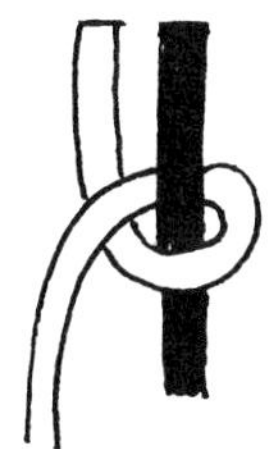

8 Knotted braid using three threads
This braid is made by knotting alternate sides with half hitches onto a central thread. First, knot the right side onto the central thread. Next, knot the left side onto the central thread. Try this with different weights of thread, eg thin threads at each side round a thick centre thread.

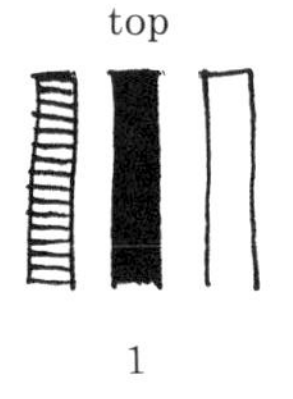

1

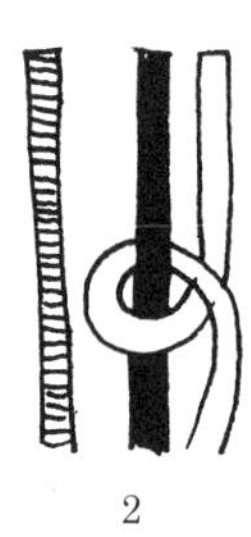

2

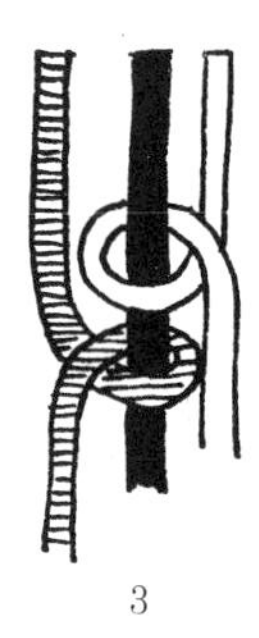

3

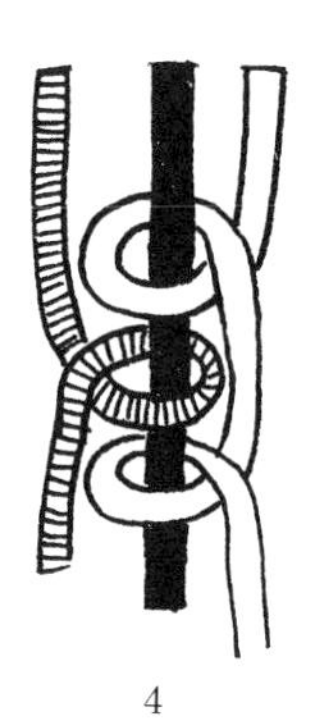

4

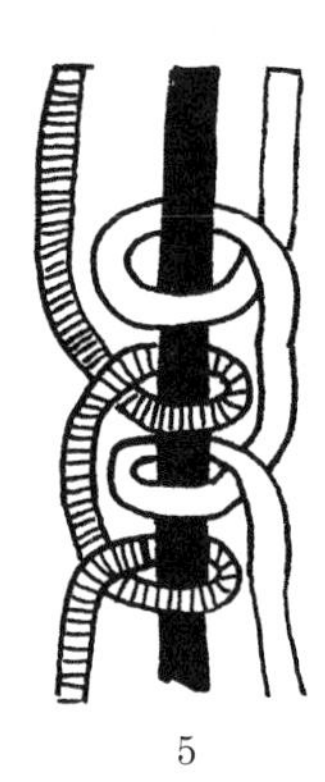

5

9 Needleweaving (see pages 38 and 79 for technique)
Braids of needleweaving can be made in any width according to the number of warps used. Tie the warps at the top, pin to a cushion or a board. Hold the warps in one hand and weave with the other. Braids like this can be woven in stripes and in any sort of thread. Try weaving yarns, for different effects. When a thread comes to an end, finish in the middle, letting the old thread fall to the back, and starting off the new thread in the same place. Darn in to finish off, later. Keep an eye on the edge of the braid to keep the tension even, and do not pull too hard on the weft. Weave a few rows, and push up with the fingers, or the eye of the needle. An interesting checked effect can be attained by leaving the weft threads, and not pushing them up. Beads can be added, threaded onto the warp threads. Weave round them as they occur. Try using strips of material like leather, corduroy, suede, knitted fabric for warps.

10 Braids made from fabric

One of the simplest ways of making a braid is to take a strip of non-woven material,* and cut out shapes along the edge.

* Felt, leather, suede. Non-woven fabric. Woven fabric can be backed with interfacing to stop fraying.

Try as many different patterns as possible, and mix straight lines with curves. If a punch is available, use that to punch holes in leather and suede strips. It is also possible to make holes by folding the strip lengthwise and cutting into the fold. Try threading fabric through the holes, too. A ruffled braid can be made by cutting a strip of jersey fabric, running a line of stitches across the middle, and gathering slightly to ruffle the material.

Interesting and unusual braids can be made with very simple stitches worked along a strip of fabric.** Cut a strip of material. The edges can also be cut and shaped. Work a line of stitches down the middle, then thread these stitches with a contrasting thread.

** Felt, wool (fray out the edges), strips of corduroy.

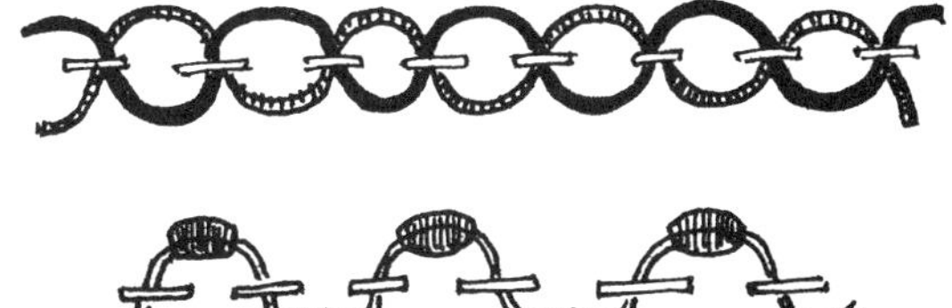

Variations on this can be achieved by adding more threaded stitches and also by adding beads. It is possible to thread several different types of thread in and out of running stitches. Also try pekinese stitch.

Tassels

Having made fringes and braids, a combination of both is a tassel. These beautiful decorations can be used in a variety of ways, or just hung in a bunch.

Take a braid or cord and tie a knot at the bottom. Take a length of fringe. Place the braid on the fringe, putting the knot just below the point where the fringe begins and glue* the braid to the fringe (see 1).

Now, carefully roll up the fringe over the braid. Either stick the end or put a little glue all the way along the top of the fringe so that it sticks as it rolls. For a fabric fringe, which might fray out round the top, fold down a couple of cms. along the top before rolling (see 3). Tassels can also be made in the same way from cut fringes made from non-woven fabric.** Narrow fringes can be combined with wide fringes to make tassels (see 4). First roll the wide fringe, then roll the narrow fringe round the top, and stick. Try to keep the rolling neat and even. A small piece of braid or decoration can also be wound round the top of the tassel (see 5). Experiment with different woven and non-woven fabric fringes to make tassels. Combine both methods. Try to make braids and cords which fit in with the tassels.

* Use as little glue as possible.

** Try felt, leather, suede, vinyl. Use jersey fabrics made of nylon, wool and rayon.

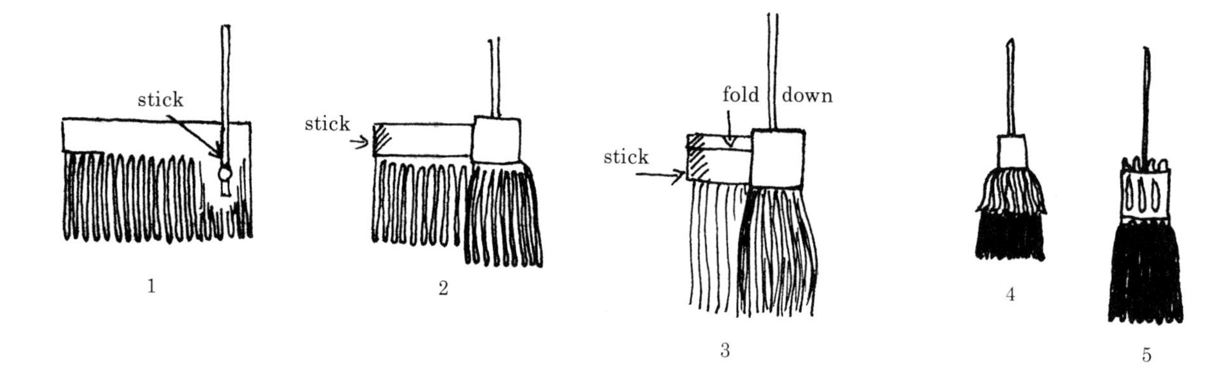

To make a tassel from thread
Take several threads about twice as long as the height of the required tassel. Fold in half and tie* with a matching thread in a knot. Leave ends (see 1). Tie a thread round the top of the bundle (see 5), and trim ends.

To make a larger tassel at the end of a cord, follow through step one (see 1). Do this again to make two bundles. Take a cord, and tie a knot at the end. Tie the ends of the two bundles round the cord above the knot (see 2 and 3).

Arrange the threads round the knot in the cord so that it does not show. Let the ends of the ties mingle with the rest. Tie a thread two or three times round the bundle (see 4) and tie with a knot. Tuck the ends down into the tassel behind the tie.

* Use a reef knot for safety (see page 41).

** Felt, jersey fabric.

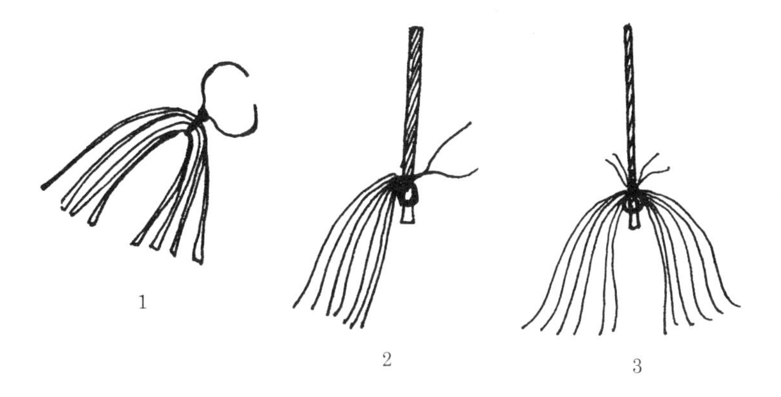

Arrange the tassel and trim the bottom threads if necessary. The size of the tassel depends on the type of thread used to make it. Try silk, wool, string, rug wool and home-made threads. Combine these and tassels on the previous page by making a thread tassel over the top of a tassel made out of a fringe. Use different colour combinations. Add fabric by taking a circle of non-woven fabric.** Cut into the edge all the way round to make a fringe, or just a jagged edge. Cut a slit (very small) in the middle (see 6). Slide onto cord above tassel (see 7). Tie (see 8). Get rid of ends of knot by threading them and pushing needle through back of fabric, and into the heart of the tassel.

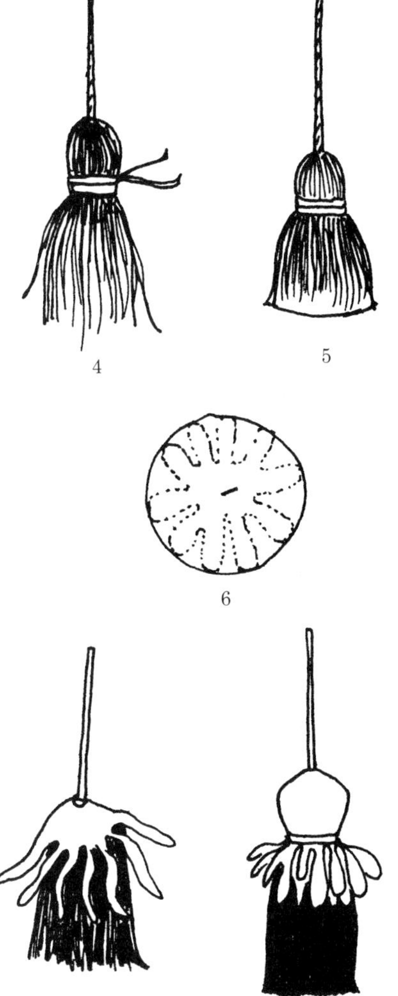

SCHOOL SUPPLIERS

E J Arnold and Son Ltd
Butterley Street
Leeds LS10 1AX

Dryad (Reeves) Ltd
Northgates
Leicester LE1 4QR

Nottingham Handcraft Limited
17 Ludlow Hill Road
Melton Road
West Bridgford
Nottingham NG2 6HD
A series of 5 sets of slides, with teacher's notes, complementary to this book and relating to work with Collage (1 set), Weaving and Needleweaving (1 set), Embroidery (2 sets), and Decorations (1 set), also obtainable from Nottingham Handcraft Limited on normal school requisition.

FURTHER READING

Embroidery for School, Joan Nicholson
Simple Canvas Work, Joan Nicholson
Dolls for Children to Make, Suzy Ives
Needle and Thread, Gisela Hein
The Zoo: Needlecraft for Young Children, Barbara Snook
Felt Gifts and Toys, Anna Griffiths
Simple Textile Dyeing and Printing, Nora Proud
Embroidery Stitches, Barbara Snook
Printing and Embroidery, Mary Newland and Carol Walklin
Inspiration for Embroidery, Constance Howard
Embroidery and Colour, Constance Howard
all published by Batsford, London.

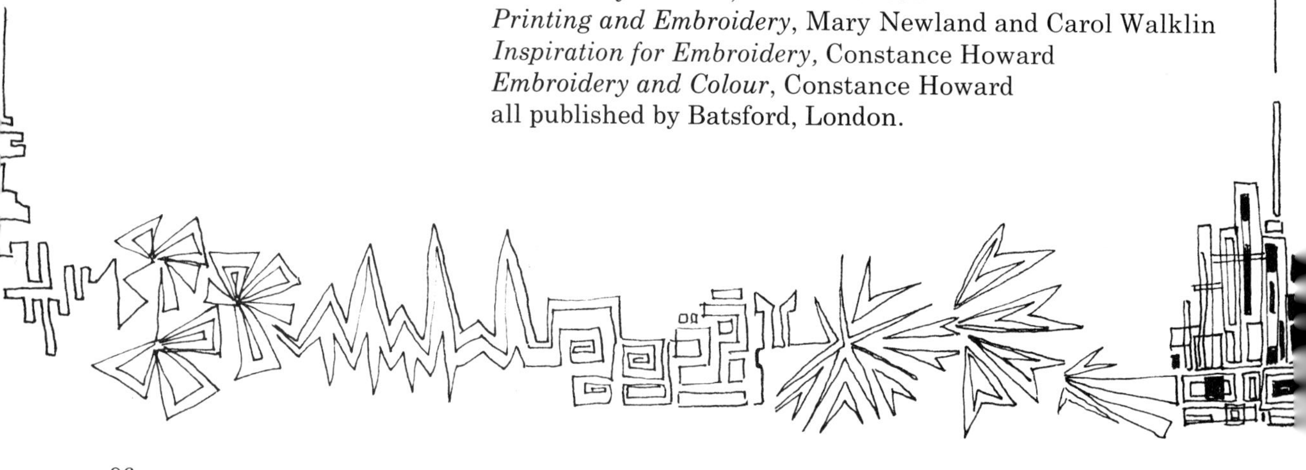